The Journey of a Wounded Healer: The Mystical Web of Mental Illness and Spirituality

Carol L. Chambers

Print ISBN: 978-1-54397-133-0

eBook ISBN: 978-1-54397-134-7

This book is dedicated to

Lois Clark and Elaine Davis, my friends who saved my life—
Marjorie Adams Beckert, my Mother, who gave me life—
and Mary Deckard Adams, my Grandmother, who showed me how
to live it—
and to all my fellow and sister travelers in this mystical web of life.

While the path may be unknown at times,
the journey is always a tender calling
from Spirit to our spirits—
a yearning to see us in sacred relationship
with the holy or transcendent,
with our precious selves, with each other,
and with the earth.
For those with Mental Illness,
the path may take unexpected, painful turns
that we do not understand.
No one's path is independent from another's;
all are nestled in the sweet manifestations
of Spirit's longing for relationship.
This book is devoted to understanding mental illness
and spirituality as interwoven in our life journey.
As we are tender with ourselves, each other,
and the earth, our kind-hearted passage in this world
can open new vistas of spiritual depth and love.

Acknowledgements

I am grateful to have survived the years of agony, torment, and brokenness that lived in my heart during the 60+ years prior to my diagnosis and appropriate treatment for significant mental illnesses. My gratitude extends to the multitude of people throughout my now 67 years of life who have befriended me, therapists who tried to do their best to help me, and physicians who attempted, successfully or not, to assist me in dealing with the myriad of physical symptoms which accompany undiagnosed significant mental illnesses. I also want to thank the medical personnel who, at long last, did discover my diagnoses and work with me through the prolonged period of developing a medication regimen.

All that being said, I am most grateful to the two women who supported me during my last and most significant episode of disintegration. Without the selfless and unconditional love of my two friends, Elaine Davis and Lois Clark, I could not have authored this book because, in one way or another, I would not have survived that episode. They taught me about love that required sacrifice and whole-hearted compassion to assure the well-being and health of another individual. In other words, they were my 'friends' in the deepest meaning possible. Additionally, their care for my precious companion, Finian, when I was unable to tend for him myself, enabled me to be about the business of healing while knowing that he was cherished by his doting 'aunts' who love him as their own. I'm also grateful for their willingness to be "proof readers", a tedious job indeed.

While many friends entered my journey along the way, Joyce Robinson has been my friend for more than 30 years and supported me in more ways than I can count throughout those decades. I am grateful for her love and friendship.

I especially want to thank Jackie McNeil who, in her willingness to consult with me (as well as provide editorial comments), encouraged me to alter the trajectory of the telling of my story which resulted in a more meaningful, readable, and valuable book as a whole. I also want to thank Kathy Gambrell for her willingness to "proof" my manuscript as well. Any mistakes that remain are solely my responsibility.

This was a difficult and, sometimes painful, book to write. I want to thank Jillian Bannon and the Celtic Spirituality Group for encouraging me for almost two years. I want to thank the Wednesday Energy Meditation Group for their initial positive reaction to my story, thus giving me the momentum to make that final 'push' toward completion. I want to thank my many friends, especially Linda Friedman, for repeatedly assuring me that my story was a story that needed telling.

I want to thank my son, David, who experienced some of the most difficult results of my living with mental illness, for unfailingly loving me and caring deeply for my well-being. He, his wife, Gina, and my two grand-children, Jackson and Emmy give me hope for the future and joy in the present.

To all those who have begun to share their stories with me as they learn of my work, thank you. We are truly 'all in this together'.

Although I know that he knows it already through my hugs and kisses, I want to thank my little 12-pound companion dog, Finian, for giving up countless long walks, playtimes, and car rides as he sat (or slept) patiently beside me as I spent hours at my computer. He brings me happiness beyond measure and companionship that sustains me in my challenging times.

Finally, I want to thank the helpful folks at Bookbaby, especially Damon Glatz, for aiding this new author in navigating the publishing process.

A VERY IMPORTANT STATEMENT TO MY READERS— Please read this before continuing: Please understand that I do not advocate to anyone that they should stop taking medications or turn away from medical or psychotherapeutic assistance. I do, indeed, utilize several forms of alternative healing and meditation techniques as an adjunct to the medical intervention that saved my life; but I am, in the strongest of words, stating that neither this book, nor my story, suggests that you should change your current medical or psychotherapeutic regimen. This book contains NO medical or psychotherapeutic advice or suggestions for change in any reader's current treatment.

TABLE OF CONTENTS

PROLOGUE

I am standing in the depths of a Florida forest, my back up against a giant cypress tree. I feel my feet firmly on the grass and dirt, rooted in the energy of Mother Earth. Sending my roots further and further down until I touch the center of Earth Energy, I am grounded. Raising my arms as high as they can go, I join with the branches of the tree, spreading out its welcome of Energy from Sky and Sun and Moon and Stars.

Feeling fully grounded and centered, I begin to create my sacred space and offer up my thanks to the six directions—North, South, East, West, the sun and starry beings up above and the guardian spirits and depth of the earth below—as I have learned to do from many traditions and here from the ancient Celts and the many tribes of Native Americans:

To the East I give thanks for the air, communication, and for the work of Spirit. I welcome Eagle, power animal of the East into the circle. I have learned to fly and soar on the back of Eagle, gaining new knowledge and insight into my place in All There Is and my calling in the world.

To the South I give thanks for fire, energy, passion, and creativity, for new beginnings and new growth, for Truth, Beauty, and Purity. Serpent, power animal of the South joins me as well. From Serpent I have learned to confront my fears, my insecurities, and my former unwillingness to 'shed my skin' of all that does not serve me well.

To the West I give thanks for water, emotion, psyche, movement, for endings and for the fulness of life. To Jaguar, power animal of the West, I give welcome and gratitude. In the eyes of Jaguar, I have begun to claim my personal power and recognize the good that power can do.

To the North I give thanks for earth, home, security, fertility, for wisdom and thought. For the perseverance of Hummingbird, power animal of the North, I give my awe and thankfulness for its example. Hummingbird teaches me of the lengths we must go to 'come home' and the journeys that we must undertake to do the same.

I welcome the power of Mother Earth who supports me and keeps me safely in my reality of all that I am and can be. I thank her for all that she shows me in the deepest part of her energy, in her pathways to places I now visit again and again to learn of new ways to heal and be healed. I welcome all the spirits of below and I welcome the beauty of the stars, sun and moon and rejoice in the upward pull to change and places of the highest learning and awareness. I give thanks to all the ancestors, ascended masters, and spirit helpers who have joined me in this circle. I welcome and am grateful to the Spirits of the ancestors, the Hidden Folk, the Land, all helping spirits who share their wisdom, healing, and unconditional love. I welcome Turtle, Maralda and Ciorcal, Guides of my ever-evolving journey. I give thanks that I am here to celebrate all of life and all of me.

Now I am ready. I sit cross-legged on the soft mossy grass in the middle of the healing circle I have created and let myself think back through the several years since my collapse. I am not 'cured'; but I have experienced more healing than I thought possible. I have learned not only to manage my disease; I have learned to love and accept my feelings and thoughts about my disease. It no longer controls my life, though it informs it. I have become able to author a book—one which chronicles my search for understanding of my disease of mental illness and its inter-relationship with my spiritual journey.

I have come to a place of great spiritual understanding that enables me to wrap the arms of my heart around my whole self. I am a wounded healer and I give thanks. For the first time in my life I am stable, and I am free. I rely on medication for the bio-chemical portion of my illness in the same way that I do for any other illnesses; and like the Shamans who came before me I celebrate the medicine that Mother Earth shares with her children.

I rejoice in all that the Source of All Energy is doing in and through me. I take time for my own healing and am tender with the symptoms that still need my love and attention from time to time, grateful to have come through it all to this day when I can touch the joy that always seemed just out of reach.

INTRODUCTION

My journey has been mysterious, wild, and liberating! My spiritual pathways have taken me from a small child struggling to live within the contradictions of good and evil, to a conservative ordained minister, and then through many paths to a home-grown, Spirit-led Shaman and Reiki Practitioner. The mental illnesses with which I live have taken me to the depths of depression, anxiety, and panic and to the highs of feeling invulnerable to the consequences of mistakes and decisions made during hypo-manic episodes, to stability and wholeness grounded within the strong branches and roots of my own Tree of Life.

While I did not fully understand it for many years, I think I instinctively knew that my search for a meaningful spiritual experience was, somehow, interwoven with my struggle with various forms of mental illness throughout my life. However, after two Masters' Degrees and 4 years of graduate study in various aspects of religion, as well as countless hours of therapy and self-reflection, I was still searching. As a person with decades of dealing with significant mental illness and one who has studied numerous spiritual traditions in depth and searched for spiritual meaning and illumination for the same number of decades, it seemed likely that I was as good a candidate as any to write such a book as this.

This book, while divided into two parts, does not necessarily fall neatly into such. What is most important for the reader to understand is that while the first section of the book may feel immensely sad, it is not a tragedy. Rather, it lays the foundation for the wonderfully positive transformation that is described in the second half of my story. The title of this book gives several important 'clues' to my perspective regarding my journey. I will speak often of my role as a 'Wounded Healer'. The story is not simple and rarely easy to understand. As I journeyed, I walked through paths of despair, anxiety, and sometimes the longing to end it all. I traveled into addiction, eating disorders and horrible consequences when my imprisoned mind made terrible decisions. I spent decades caught in the confusing journey of treatment, through disappointment and betrayal by a system that always seemed to fall short of providing me with what I really needed. Most of all, I longed for life to make sense. Eventually, writing became my first healer.

Many have asked me about the purpose of this book. And it is Hope. Not all, and perhaps few, will resolve their sense of wholeness in the ways that I have. I am not some guru of mental illness and sacred transformation. What I desire to do with this book is to simply encourage others (and those who love or work with them) to be open to looking at mental illness and spirituality in ways beyond their earlier understanding. That is all I did—I opened my mind to looking at my mental illness as a spiritual gift and my sacred transformation as a way to expand my knowledge of mental illness. I returned to the truths of my youth—those truths I discovered before I became convinced that I was a damaged person.

I am a 'wounded healer'; I have always been a healer, always had access to the energy of the universe; and, experienced my first 'wounding' when I was little more than an infant. Many spiritual healers believe that wounding is integral in the gift of healing. This woundedness is, indeed, how the energy and the desire to heal others seeped and crashed into my soul. I still struggle with the effects of this woundedness; and, particularly, the life-long nature of the wounds themselves and the profound impact those wounds have had on my life. I long to be financially secure, more in control of the darkness that still follows me and to find a way to 'fix' the broken relationships along the way. Even so, I know this woundedness is still playing itself out in my life and that with each passing day, the meaning becomes clearer, though not always easier to bear. Being a wounded healer means that my life will reflect those wounds; and, perhaps, new ones. Nevertheless, it is the woundedness that gives me strength, courage, and energy to turn my sorrow into compassion, and my love into healing.

This book is a gift—a 'coming out' of the shadows of complicity with others' expectations and beginning to live my own truth and claim my own story. This story tells of the transformation of unrelenting pain—spiritual, mental, and physical—into a wholeness that allows me to fulfill my calling from the Universe and live in healthy and fulfilling ways. My journey is of a spiraling nature. The spirals of mental illness interweave within a web of experiences that are sometimes frightening, dangerous or wonderfully healing and whole. The spirals of Transcendence, Love, Light and the Sacred that lives within my soul are there as well. In the telling of my story it became important to describe the connection between two significant spirals—the realities of my life events and my ever-changing understanding of the spiritual aspects of my life. Obviously, one cannot truly be separate from the other, but clarity demands some method of describing the interconnection within the mystical web so that the overlapping and interacting of one spiral with another is not lost.

There is nothing in this book that indicates that one method of healing is better than or superior to another. There is also no suggestion that one cannot practice multiple traditions at the same time. I have tried to instill a basic sense of non-judgment, of mutual acceptance and absolute respect. I honor all journeys and believe that all pathways (except those which are dark with negative or hurtful energy) are valuable and life-sustaining.

Parts of this book were incredibly difficult to write. As much as I would have liked to skip over all the painful and downright embarrassing aspects of my life, that would not be speaking my truth. In my journey, I constantly need to remind myself that in the entirety of it, I must find and keep an attitude of tenderness toward myself, those with whom I travel this journey, the earth, the past and the future. To hold someone or something compassionately is to cradle it in my hands, to seek and find the beauty and truth that speaks only to me. To be tender with myself and all my possibilities means to be open, to rule nothing out except that which is hurtful to myself or others, and to hold each opportunity gently, waiting for the beauty and truth to speak to my soul. This is the 'tender journey' and it awaits. I have made a commitment to be especially soothing, kind-hearted, and loving as I travel through these intersecting and overlapping spirals.

As I tell this story two things are crucial in my survival of my latest and my most desperate downward spiral. First, I had the unfailing support of two wonderful women who, quite simply, enabled me to endure my darkest period. Few are blessed to have friends give up months of their life to care for you (and your dog) and provide you with a safe place to live and heal. They advocated for me when I could not advocate for myself and kept me wrapped close in a cloak of safety. They remain my primary source of support even now.

Secondly, I am an educated white woman of privilege. As I surfaced from the worst of my despair, I was able to research my illness and ask critical questions of mental health providers. I came to trust myself to say "no" to questionable drugs. I eventually could differentiate between helpful interventions and non-helpful ones. Federally subsidized health insurance supplied my medical care and I was living on my social security and pension so that even though life was indescribably difficult, I had enough 'advantages' to negotiate my way through a confusing and inadequate system. Many, if not most, people with profound mental illness do not have any of this in their lives. As this reality became increasingly obvious, it required me to begin a new and necessary spiritual journey that played out in my commitment to give back to my community, my friends, and my fellow and sister travelers. It is in this spirit that I authored this book.

PART ONE

1

Spinning the Web

I peer up, eyes nearly swollen shut from my days of early morning crying, then my shaking, trembling fear throughout the day followed by the excruciating anxiety of succumbing to sleep, knowing that when I awake, I must do it all again. I cannot see the top of this, my steepest spiral; I can only feel and hear the rush of the water in the swirling waterspout in which I appear captured. Pieces of my shattered life spin around my head causing me to duck and hide as much as I can. I know from past experience that, if I can find my way home, I may ever so slowly feel myself lifted from this barren emptiness of despair to increasing light and hope. But, for now, I am not there—I simply am not there. Through days of despair I fumble and fall, unable to reach even the next level of this spiral that holds me while I plead for the strength to find myself amid the roar of the mis-firings of my brain and the catastrophic storm taking place in my spirit and heart. But now, at this time, if not for the despair, I would not exist at all. I am bereft.

I felt as though I was spinning in the vortex of a tornado. I was a large rock that rapidly dropped to the ground when the tornado blew itself out. I collapsed as I spun downward in the gravity of despair and I could not brace myself for the fall. All that I knew for sure was that I was 63 years old, more fragile in every way than I had ever been before and far less able to access hope or determination. It was different from other times that I have traveled the darker side of this journey. Since I was much older and unemployed, I was much less independent and much closer to calling it quits. This time the unrelenting anxiety, the hopeless depression, and the longing for an end to it all forced me to begin to ask some questions, allow myself to listen and take steps to bring some insight into what was happening to me.

It took two years for me to fully understand the nature of the interwoven web of mental illness and spirituality and to be able to embrace the whirling, spinning spirals within that web which have been my home as far back as I can remember. This 'bottom' of the spiral is where I most often make my decisions, where I have made them before, and where I hope that I never have to make them again. But the nature of my life journey tells me this is something I may have to do. It is a reality that keeps me both grateful and terrified in the same breath.

The differences now are many and significant. Unlike other death dealing spirals of anxiety and depression that I have encountered my whole life; I am not alone. I am lonely beyond measure, but I am not alone. And my decision is made—I do not want to fail to surface from this deep and fearful place, although I know that failure is still possible. Nevertheless, I now have a diagnosis after living in the netherworld of unknown and unidentified mental illness since I was barely a teenager. My life has been a series of spirals down, and then up, up, and then down.

The spirals throughout my six decades are many. But, unlike other times, now I can see a twin spiral weaving in and out of the mystical web that records my life's story. Spiritual in nature, this web has protected me, led me in new paths and saved me for these better times. Intertwined with the storms of the ins and outs and ups and downs of the living of my life is a sweet sense of Spirit who calls to me in tender ways to follow my journey. Some spiral pathways have been vicious and life-threatening and some less so. But, regardless of those spirals—some terrifying and some not so much—Spirit has always accompanied me on my journey although most of the time I did not and could not see it.

This web is always in motion. I experience my mental illness within the spirals of my spirituality at times; and, at times it is my spirituality that dances within the spirals of mental illness. These trans-formations occur on a daily, even hourly basis. Most of all, what is true for me is that each one informs, embraces, and welcomes the other and the two aspects of my soul are so intertwined that separation is not possible, nor desirable.

Because I now understand that the web of my journey is built of these interlocking spirals, I would not seek to separate them. It is the capacity to see one within the other that has brought me the under-standing for which I have longed and, more importantly, the willing-ness and excruciatingly painful ability to slowly reach rung after rung of the upward spiral. Each step forward brings its own lesson and each slip backwards reminds me that I am not ready for the up and I am thrown slightly back down to learn both mentally and spiritually what I have thus far missed. My pace is slow, and my peace is not perfect, nor is it constant, but I can now recognize when the Universe surrounds me with the opportunity of finding my way into a calming dance of Love and Light and I can, most of the time, choose to come home to the center of my being. It remains hard, sometimes overwhelmingly so; the swirling and whirling of my earlier difficult and painful times sometimes still call to me and sometimes overtakes me with little to no warning.

And, so, this is the story of my weaving through this mystical, sometimes magical web-like journey—a journey which included many creative outlets, scholarly pursuits, successful careers, and fluctuations in spiritual outlooks. It also included months and years of darkness, dysfunctional relationships, disintegration, and hopelessness. Many of these aspects of my journey occurred simultaneously which made my steps often tentative and faltering, caught in a knot of confusion and longing. Like a circling, whirling dancer spinning around a room, I could only see one part of the room at a time. My weaving and spinning suffered from that limitation; and, that made it difficult for me to process, much less, integrate my entire environment all at once. So, there I was, stuck in these zig-zagging spinning spirals of change, uncertainty, and chaos. As the years wore on, I grew somewhat accustomed to the out-of-control feelings and behaviors in which I seemed to be stuck, but I was never able to slow down the whirling enough so that I could seek understanding, acceptance and, perhaps, stability.

It is not that I didn't try, but it was rarely possible for me to identify exactly when my journey was spiraling down into the storm of depression or spinning back to the top. Until one day, it all stopped at just the time when I was weaving my way down to utter darkness and I was left dazed, confused, and very, very scared.

I began this difficult journey, at least as much as I can remember of it, when I was seventeen and a junior in high school. I was never a happy teen, never felt comfortable in my own skin and never saw the way out of a life that caused me to tremble in constant fear and unworthiness. I was doing all I could to keep the façade in place; and then, suddenly, seemingly out of nowhere, I became a desperate, lonely teenager, sitting on my bed screaming "God, what is wrong with me?" Since no one, certainly not God, could give me an answer, I decided that 'I' was what was wrong with me. As a life-long believer in the healing power of God through Jesus Christ, this period of dark and aimless screaming took hold and would haunt me for decades to come. I came to understand, or thought I did, that this darkness would always be with me and that love was far away and unlikely to appear on the horizon any time soon. I eventually went back to school; but I was a changed person, deprived of what little childhood I had left and thrust into a constant and unrelenting search for meaning and purpose. This search took me down many roads, some of them quite 'spiritual' in a conventional sort of way, others completely beyond what my traditional 'religious upbringing' would accept, and some simply dangerous, but I was unable to see any connection at all.

The telling of my most recent disintegration and then the first sets the stage for the recording of my story. My journey as I perceive it has been one of chaos and spirit and weaving within the mystical web of mental illness and sacred transformation. Weaving that I rarely understood caused me to spin (sometimes out of control) down maelstroms into deep, dark depression and anxiety and then up the cyclones into what felt like 'normal'. My primary diagnosis is Bipolar 2, so I am not a person who experienced or experiences extraordinary highs, so for me the upward spirals, for the most part, ended at level ground. This does not mean that I didn't experience manic or hypo-manic behaviors because I did (and, sometimes still do), but, during those 'highs' I did not feel euphoria, unlimited energy, or joy. Instead, my mind was always spinning from place to place, hoping to fall into that sweet, secret, or so it seemed, place of compassion and peace. For decades I continued to weave and career, sometimes slowly meandering through the oftentimes confusing webs that appeared before me. Other times I felt as if I were spinning as fast as any human could, though still not arriving where I thought I wanted to be. In addition to Bipolar 2, my other diagnoses include Generalized Anxiety Disorder, PTSD and Panic Disorder.

When I first envisioned the nature of this book and began to create the format in its infancy, I landed on three aspects of life that I longed to understand—authenticity, coherence, and transcendence. While this choice does not neatly divide itself into three parts, those three words still hold the deepest meaning for my long and painstaking exploration of the endless spirals that exist throughout my life story. I do not believe that I was ever consciously inauthentic. Though I did not know my diagnoses at the time, I now know that I was, indeed, acting authentically within the journey in which I lived. The search for coherence was the great motivator and great burden I carried through the first six decades of my life. I never stopped looking for the secret map that would make my life make sense, to lead me to coherence. I do not mean that I was or appeared to be incoherent (although sometimes I'm sure I was) but that my life itself did not have coherence—the wholeness that I believed life was supposed to have.

Finally, as I worked my way through and out of my most critical time of crisis, I understood at a profound level that there is no one way to describe or understand transcendence. It took a willingness—a personally dangerous and costly willingness—to go beyond the teachings of my childhood and practices of my adulthood and look for a way to explore and combine many traditions, beliefs, and practices into a sense of wholeness that brought the peace for which I had longed and sought for six decades. This journey does not mean that I am always able to maintain that peace throughout episodes of despair or mania, but it is there waiting for me when I am able to access it. I wrote this in the beginning of my journal in May 1993: "A woman's special gift to herself is the passion that gives birth to the willingness to embrace her deepest, most wounded self and journey until the pain is transformed into power and rage becomes one with change." Even then, though I did not know where it would lead, I was looking for transformation, understanding and power to change and grow.

I am of Irish heritage and while the Celtic tradition is not the only tradition that utilizes the 'Tree of Life' as a means of exploring the many worlds in which we live, the knowledge of this Tree of Life began to give me center and enlightenment that proved to be pivotal in my future processing of my spiraling journeys. It is the center which holds the pathways together. As will become more obvious along the way, the branches, roots, and trunk of the tree all have distinct yet interweaving roles in understanding the coming together of the various spirals in which I lived, moved, and navigated my confusing and bewildering life. Initially what seemed most important was the knowledge that roots do not tangle and twist down into the earth merely to create some underground tunnel of abstract art, but rather to gain the nutrients that the uppermost branches need to continue their journey into the sky. In the middle of it all, the trunk—center of the tree--pulls both upper and lower tree-worlds together into a whole that is so strong that it will survive even the fiercest of storms.

Initially, I focused only on the upward and downward spirals of this great tree and overlooked the sturdiness that was ever-present in the chest of the tree where security and reality lived. I remained stuck in the highs and lows completely missing the quiet center of peace and strength. I do not believe that the trunk of the tree worries about holding up the branches of the trees or gathering together the maze of its roots. It just knows that both are integral to the very nature of 'tree-ness'. It would take me a long time to bring my tree of life into the world in which I live.

2

Illuminating the Web

When I began to finally deal with the fact that I had a 'mental illness' I truly had no idea what that meant. As strange as it sounds for a person who had worked my entire life in various helping professions, counseling people in various settings; and, eventually taking on the pastoral care of an entire congregation, I did not know what it meant for me. I certainly knew or thought I knew what it appeared to mean for others. I could identify behaviors and symptoms and I even sought help for my own depression. But, mental illness—I think not! Though I felt only compassion for those with whom I came in contact who were struggling with mental illness, I could not find that compassion for myself. I stood at the top of a cliff looking down into the spiral that would lead me to some understanding of my own battle and found that same fear I believe I would feel if someone talked me into bungee jumping. I was standing on the platform with no belief in the strength of the cable or that I would bounce back up and find some gentle landing.

In my brief discussion of the nature of the use of the term mental illness in the telling of my story it is important to remember that there are many conditions included in the umbrella term 'mental illness'. While it would be possible to apply the insights of my story to many other diagnoses, I can be the most forthcoming and authentic when I focus on my own diagnoses which include: Bipolar Disorder 2 (a Mood Disorder), Generalized Anxiety Disorder, Panic Disorder, and PTSD.

Although I cannot speak with significant knowledge about psychopathology, I can speak of my frustration about the impact sociopathic behaviors and actions have on general feelings towards me as I attempt to share my own experience with others. Some people believe that because I have a mental illness, I may well be capable of (or even prone to) sociopathic behaviors because society tends to confuse the distinction between sociopathic characteristics and mental illness. Fortunately, many people are becoming educated about mental illness and have begun to understand the differences between the diagnoses and behaviors. While my story includes various forms of treatment that I tried before and after diagnosis (later ones more successful, earlier ones—not as much), I was fortunate to live in communities where I was able, for the most part, to be 'safe'.

While I try to refrain from judging those who choose not to pursue treatment except in those cases where the lack of treatment leads to danger to others or the environment, their behavior has a direct impact on public perception of a population that includes me, and I am disappointed. I also know that at least half of those who struggle with mental illness have no access to treatment and I want to find ways to provide them with love, support and some means to seek treatment. This desire is profoundly spiritual and knowing that I cannot do that yet fills me with sadness but also gives me hope and a longing to discover an approach which will help change that reality.

To fully tell my story, I must briefly describe the various forms of mental illness that comprise my diagnosis. Individually, they form the vortices which overlap in the multi-faceted swirling rings I now lovingly claim as the spirals of my life. Most researchers including the American Psychiatric Association suggest that 'while mental illness can occur at any age, three-fourths of all mental illness begins by age 24'.[1] This was certainly true for me as my first real descent into unexplained mental illness happened as I described before when I was 17. As I went through school few understood the battle I was facing; and, most did not even realize that I was facing it. I did not speak of it, tried to hide it, and made every attempt to live as if I did not struggle with the deadening 'lows' and the confusing 'highs' that plagued my life on an almost constant basis. It's hard enough to be a teenager in the best of circumstances, I would have settled for anything other than what I was feeling.

Although I have several diagnoses, I suppose that Bipolar 2 is the most significant of them but, quite frankly, it may depend on the day. Because my diagnoses are complex it is difficult to separate one from another. However, they are separate diagnoses. Bipolar Disorders are 'Mood Disorders'. As with any diagnosis, these disorders exist on a continuum. To further complicate this diagnosis, there are two types of Bipolar diagnoses. Unlike Bipolar 1 which has profound 'highs' along with significant 'lows', Bipolar 2 has comparable depths of depression and despair but the manic period is referred to as hypomania where behaviors are less extreme but may be just as dangerous and self-destructive. Some of my behaviors during my hypo-manic phases of living with this diagnosis led to terrible life-altering decisions—the negative impacts, in some cases, affect me still today. The depressive episodes can last for years. Mania rarely lasts as long as the depression does. Bipolar 2 can also be 'rapid cycling' which means that the time between highs and lows is very brief. I am diagnosed with rapid cycling Bipolar and the changes in moods can be akin to multiple whiplashes—with little to no time to recover in between.

Generalized Anxiety Disorder--anxiety that affects every aspect of my behavior is also among my diagnoses. I have found that many people are often anxious about specific events in their lives. However, Generalized Anxiety Disorder renders me unable to escape constant anxiety and it is rarely linked to a specific event, although particularly stressful events may have a significant impact on the level of anxiety I am experiencing.

I am grateful the public has a better understanding of PTSD (post-traumatic stress disorder) because of the work of the U.S. military to understand the effects of war-time trauma on returning soldiers. While this work was occurring, researchers also observed that PTSD could affect anyone who has experienced significant trauma at some point in their lives. The most common symptom of PTSD is the 'flashback' where the mind is suddenly consumed by events experienced in the past. Unfortunately, persons suffering from PTSD cannot differentiate between the present and past experiences at the time and these interruptions from the past make it exceedingly difficult to live a wholly stable life. My worst period of the experience of flashbacks was in my 30's when I first began to come to terms with the sexual and physical abuse I endured as a child at the hands of my father. Later, although I certainly never expected it, I also experienced and still experience flashbacks from this last, most difficult, descent into despair and anxiety.

Panic Disorder can appear in the middle of some simple activity. Panic can overcome me, and I have no idea where it came from. All I know is that I cannot breathe, my heart races and I feel completely out of control. While many do end up in the ER, I was and am so terrified of medical intervention that I taught myself to stay present while the worst of it passed. Eventually, I learned some breathing methods which helped a great deal but the out of control spiraling (neither down nor up—just caught in the whirlwind) is debilitating while it is occurring. Medication that deals with the physical aspects of Panic Attacks (though not the emotional ones) was finally added to the medical portion of my varied toolbox. This medication has greatly reduced the incapacitating effects of these unpredictable and debilitating events. No mental illness fits neatly in a box. Even a diagnosis does not mean that every individual with that same diagnosis will look and act the same. I learned this myself when quite early after receiving a diagnosis, I began to read book after book on Bipolar 2. Not all were useful, but some gave me some important insights.

In the midst of discussing the spiraling nature of mental illness I cannot ignore my simultaneous spiraling experience with Spirit. If I could intertwine the two and still render the words comprehensible I would. I can't. I tried. I can only speak authentically of my own experience. Earlier in my life my description would have been traditional. I would have tried to keep it 'acceptable' and worked hard so as not to offend or upset anyone. That never served me well. Over the last decade or so I have come to describe Spirit differently as I have become freer from the constrictions I put on myself in the past. I paid a heavy price for making that transformation, but it was that transformation that made it possible for me to survive spiritually, physically, and mentally.

In a world where things are often made more complex than they are, I learned there is great wisdom in understanding that the Sacred is, simply, All There Is. I had long labored under the false impression that one day I would 'make it' spiritually. That might include acting or feeling a certain way. I even thought I knew what I would look like—my face, always glowing—just like a Sunday School teacher who I worshipped at 5. Now, beyond the fact that this is simply not true, the problem in such thinking led me to stagnation. As long as I focused on this early notion of spirituality, I quashed any attempt by Spirit to speak to me in new and exciting ways. After decades of believing that there was only one way to experience God, I learned that by limiting and fearing my openness I deprived my spirit (little 's') miraculous and wonderful variations of sacred encounters as Spirit tenderly led me both deeper and higher. Because I worked so hard to *become* spiritual, I missed that I simply *was* spiritual. The Sacred is within.

I call the Divine by many names: God, Spirit, Grandmother, Shakti, Light, Life Force, and so on. While my experience with Spirit is extremely meaningful to me; wisdom comes in knowing that my experience may well not be the least bit meaningful to someone else. All I want to share with another person is that this Source beyond me enables me to live another way—a way where peace is not based on conformity, but on universal acceptance and love.

I particularly appreciate the definition of Spirit by Gerry C. Stearns in his book, *Power Animals*. "…Spirit—that energy that enfolds you, moves through you, guides and responds to you—is always with you. There is never one moment in which you are separated from that Power. You are a part of it, and it is an integral part of you. Even in those times when you may feel completely alone, you are intimately connected to Spirit. The universe and all that is within it is Spirit, including you. You are a being of Spirit—a being of energy—and as such you are constantly connected to everything else."[2] I use the words 'tender' and 'gentle' a lot. For I believe that is the nature of Spirit. Spirit leads in ways that embrace me. Spirit enfolds me and encompasses me in grace and lives in my struggles (even when I do not or cannot see it). In ways beyond my wildest longings, if I welcome that infusion of love, I will rest inside Spirit as creation cradled by Creator.

When my pain threatens to overwhelm me—and it does at times, I have no choice but to throw open my arms and allow Spirit to speak in whatever way I can hear. Many times, throughout my struggles I sought a spirituality outside of myself. I tried new practices and sometimes forgot that it is not the new practice that made me spiritual; though the practice did enable me to access Spirit in new ways. It is a fine line to walk, but one that is important as I continue my tender journey toward fully connecting with Spirit who already permeates my very being. Practices are always just paths to the Way. I finally celebrated my inner desire to burn bright with the passionate Light that lives within and fills my heart with yearning for the Holy. Until I came to understand that all that I sought is within my heart and spirit, I was unable to experience the Great Spirit—union with the Universe and All There Is.

There are moments when my somewhat literal mind longs for an easy description of 'God'. However, the simple description that I learned in Sunday School decades ago no longer 'works' for me. As I came to better understand the nature of Spirit, I began to know myself as the center of the circle I call 'God' or 'Spirit' or 'Light'—the circumference so large that it extends into infinity. While it may exceed human capacity to understand infinity, I find myself in a circle of light or energy or pure power radiating virtually forever from where I stand

and from where others stand. That same glow of energy, Spirit, who is present in my innermost heart bursts forth in all directions. And as my circle of Divine Energy melds and molds with others, Love is born.

For me, Spirit speaks in Nature. It is not just about enjoying the sights, smells and sounds of nature as wonderful as those gifts are; it is about being in the one place where nothing distracts my spirit from hearing Great Spirit. It is about truly touching the ground—literally touching the ground with nothing but perhaps fallen leaves between my feet and the earth itself. It is about returning to that from which I came and to where I will go at the close of my current time on the earth. This is home—Nature—this is what sustains me. This is where I experience the Tree of Life on a physical plane. I can lean against such a tree and experience deep in my body all that I encounter in my spirit. Coming to joyful acceptance of the gifts of the Great Mother and basking in them, I find my way to myself.

Because my human existence is connected to Spirit, the Source of all energy, and of being itself, I will not remain alive if I am separate from this Source. What I can be and certainly have been is unaware of this connection. And is this not the journey itself? When I connect with my own breath, I come closer to knowing the truth of the greater connection. And when I do so in the center of a forest full of trees—real or imagined—I feel my breath extend down the roots into the earth and up through the branches into the sky above, I can begin to absorb, on the human side, the connectedness of earth, air, sky, breath, and energy itself. In that infinite stillness I experience God, Light, and Life. There is no beginning and no end; no separation at all. As I expand my heart throughout my journey here on this earth, I gradually--oh, so gradually--wind my way into deeper and deeper consciousness of this connectedness until I know that all of us are indeed One.

And so, when my heart is touched, when my human spirit is lifted, when hope is restored or at least glimpsed, I am in the very presence of Something Greater. When indeed I experience this Something Greater, I am, at the core of my being, spiraling into connection with Spirit or Source—that inner Sacred Spark simply waiting to be lit. Every time I encounter Spirit, I remind myself that it is a connection I feel—the connection of my own Divine nature with All That Is. I struggle often with this connection. Perhaps I simply cannot grasp in human terms what I already know--that the Sacred resides in me and is me. Sacred Spirit calls to me to look inside—deep inside—for the very spirit of Truth and Beauty.

3

Seeking the Web

This is my story. It is lengthy (after all, I've now lived 67 years), it is complex, and much of it is sad and painful. It always lies within the mystical web of my life—sometimes obvious, sometimes hidden even from my own thinking. When I experienced my most serious collapse some of my friends and family questioned how this 'happened all of a sudden'. Although this maelstrom followed a tumultuous time in my life and some simply assumed that I had just disappeared into a cave of isolation and confusion, I hope that the exploration which follows begins to describe the interlocking nature of the spirals of spiritual understanding and of life events. And although I cannot claim that I always understood the connections at the time, it is crucial that I explore these two spirals as they played out in the mystical web of inter-connection even from the earliest years of my life.

Insights (even if later) into the interweaving nature of the two aspects of my life played an important role as I sought to understand both my journey in the spiraling world of mental illness and the events in my life which led to spiritual awakening and either grew over time or were revealed in my work in the realms of higher consciousness to bring understanding, wholeness and peace. There are several traditions that have affected my life-long journey (whether I was consciously aware of them or not at the time) and they have provided additional and expanded opportunities for significant understanding since my diagnosis and appropriate medical treatment. This treatment, though difficult at times, combined all the coping skills I was developing on my own, and gave me the distance and stability so that I am able to write such a book as this. This autobiography of sorts enabled me to pull together my story within the context of a spiritual life rife with quite considerable changes in perspective and outlook. In the telling of this, my story, I have learned that my past informs my present, but it does not hold me captive. The past sets the stage and then, when I have mined all I need from it, I set it aside until I require some small part to illuminate an event down the road. Because I live my journey within mental illness—its transitions of mood, ability to cope and the effects of medication—gaining this insight was more difficult than it might have been otherwise.

When I began to reflect upon my various and distinct pathways of spirituality, I realized that since I was raised, for the most part, and trained entirely in more conservative Christian communities, it might be the better choice to describe my journey within traditional Christianity separately, since it will surface at other times throughout my story. I want to emphasize, however, that I do not see it as separate from the rest of my spiritual journey. It is, however, important to speak of the profound impact this tradition had on my life over years and years of practice.

I learned the very first time I opened my laptop to begin my then simplistic exploration regarding spirituality and mental illness that books about faith (primarily mainline and evangelical Christianity) most often deal with the ability of 'God' to heal (in other words, change or 'cure') mental illness. In fact, when I began my search on the internet for resources and used the words 'spirituality' and 'mental illness' or 'depression' in my search I found that these types of books or articles are more commonly listed than any other genre. When looked at in the context of living with mental illness, the problem with these resources, for the most part, lies in the prevailing assumption that if healing does not come, it is somehow due to lack of faith of the one for whom healing is required. When that healing does not occur, hopelessness, sorrow, and 'shame' increases.

This assumption is not unique to mental illness but that is someone else's book to write. I do not intend to imply that all books written from the Christian perspective fall into this category. Some do not. Increasingly, writers from less conservative and more liberal positions are now authoring books that raise questions about these assumptions. Unfortunately, I was not exposed to them at the time they would have been useful and so I did not include them in my discussion of that which impacted my past journey. While I acknowledge that the more conservative books, sermons, and teachings may be useful for many of my fellow/sister journeyers, that perspective did not serve me well.

Eventually, I walked away from most of organized Christianity although I believe that the teachings of Jesus are sacred and grant me great insight into the true spiritual life. This distancing of myself from Evangelical and dogmatic Christianity continues even now. For me, this specific discussion may be the most cynical in the book; but that 'cynicism' arises from the guilt and shame that resulted for me in the midst of trying to be a 'good Christian'.

This led to feelings of overwhelming unworthiness and separation from the Divine. These same beliefs neither resonated with me or contributed to my health or wholeness. This does not mean that at certain times in my life, they were not meaningful. They were indeed. But the fact that I had to strive to overcome the guilt and shame I endured when this belief system did not 'heal me' caused me great psychic and spiritual pain throughout at least the first four decades of my life. My return to Christian ministry re-ignited some of these feelings but by then I had begun to question the source of the assumptions and was somewhat less consumed by them.

While I do not remember anyone specifically suggesting my depression or anxiety came directly from my lack of faith (until I became active in the Charismatic movement) they did not have to. The Bible stories I learned as a young child all emphasized that healing comes by way of faith in Jesus. In the mind of a malleable child it was easy to believe the reverse was also true. There are so many stories of Jesus healing people because of their faith that they need no repetition here. Because Mental illness was not a separate concept at the time of Jesus, specific identification of such illnesses does not appear. There is, however, great emphasis on the healing from demons, seizures, and other so-called bizarre behaviors any of which could have included the symptoms of mental illness. Because stories of situations when healing did not occur do not appear in recorded scriptures, we do not know that Jesus specifically drew a connection between lack of healing and lack of faith; but his followers, centuries later certainly did.

My experience with Evangelical Christianity as it related to my mental illness has several parts: I believed that if faith in Jesus healed those who asked than surely if healing did not occur, it was because the person did not believe. This belief was fueled by the Biblical passages (both Old and New Testament) that said humankind is healed by the suffering of the Messiah (and in the New Testament that was Jesus). Jesus healed thousands of people according to the writers of the Gospels and it was difficult for my questioning mind to process this. As early as 5 or 6, I wondered why God allowed such dreadful things to happen to me, why I was so afraid of everything and why my Mommy was so sad so much of the time. As I grew older and more unable to take part in social activities the way I wanted to, I had no choice but to assume that only God knew what was wrong with me and 'He' wasn't telling me anytime soon. The connection of my spiritual experiences was related to the experiences of my chaotic young life, but they did not explain them. While the linkage of these spirals is obvious now, I had no hint of understanding at the time.

When I experienced my first breakdown at age 17, I asked only one question: "God, what is wrong with me?" I never got the answer; and I began what would be an almost life-long yearning for the answer to that very question. Because of the emphasis on faith in Jesus as a means of healing, I could only assume what was wrong with me was that I didn't believe hard enough. As my story will illustrate, I did everything I could to be what I thought God wanted me to be. This meant I spent hours in church activities and even eventually began a gospel singing ministry. None of this really 'worked' for me and my original despair greatly worsened because I did not have the proof everyone else seemed to have in their lives that God loved me and wanted me to be whole. I could describe this period in my life as a time when I tried to force the intertwining of the two spirals, although it is impossible that I understood this at the time.

This greatly exacerbated my belief that I was a fraud and I lived terrified that people would find out I could not experience healing by faith. In college, I tried a new avenue—the Charismatic Movement. Here the insistence on faith in Jesus' ability to heal was paramount. If you did not experience healing from whatever ailment you had, the judgment was subtle but brutal. Since I remained depressed and suicidal, I was hopelessly in despair about my latest attempt to find something, anything, which would end my pain.

A return to more mainline Christianity, albeit in a conservative denomination, did little to assuage my brokenness. It was not until I was in Seminary that I learned that other Christians, some quite famous, also suffered from ongoing depression. This supplied some much-needed relief, but my lack of healing weighed heavily on my mind. Marriage followed; and my depression was so severe I thought I might die. Again, Christianity offered no hope for me and I told very few people I was depressed because of fear of rejection. I did not yet understand others were depressed and hiding it as well; and I felt different from other 'believers' in every way. In my early 30's I simply gave up believing I could be healed. Thinking that this would free me from guilt, I just accepted that my life would never be 'normal' whatever that meant.

In reality though, I could not bring myself to give up on the practice of Christianity as the path to healing. So, for a while, I tried to push it as far to the back of my mind as I could. I did not encounter anyone who helped me understand healing in a Christian context outside of faith and devotion to Jesus. In fact, being told to pray, to let go and let God, or to turn it over to God was simply not beneficial. This advice was, indeed, extremely painful as I struggled to find curative measures in a theology that seemed to have deserted me. Strangely enough, given all my 'churchly' activities during this time, this may have been the time when the two spirals were the farthest apart—perhaps barely touching at all.

Throughout life, but particularly when my now ex-husband and I finally divorced, and my son eventually lived with his father, the guilt which consumed me was certainly inspired, at least on an unconscious level, by the theology I had made my own throughout my life. It would be many years before I could consciously work through all the issues my religious upbringing had brought into my heart and soul. Approximately four years after I was ordained, the Southern Baptist Convention decided women should not be ordained. My disappointment (even though in the end it did not affect my ordination) in what I perceived to be sexist steps on the part of the denomination in which I served pretty much freed me from trying to participate in conservative denominations, but the guilt lingered.

Off and on throughout the years that intervened between ordination and my final collapse I would return to the religion of my childhood and young adulthood hoping to find the answer to a question I didn't even know how to phrase. I only knew that guilt and shame lurked in the back of my heart; and, it never once occurred to me that perhaps this was not the path the Universe intended for me. Because the beliefs of mainline Christianity seemed to give others life-giving joy and peace, I believed, long after I needed to, that my experience was woefully out of sync with my perception regarding what being a Christian really meant.

Even now I have difficulty expressing all these things and find myself wanting to assure those I love who are practicing Christians that I mean no disrespect and that I am not questioning the role of Christianity in their lives. And, indeed, that is all true. My ongoing experience of rejection because of everything I have written above is very real and I understand that writing it honestly and authentically may subject me to further rejection. I have paid dearly in many ways for moving beyond the faith tradition that was dominant throughout most of my life. I have always hoped that people could somehow allow others to believe what they believe without any judgment. I have, to be truthful, had little experience with that being the case. Nevertheless, I maintain the hope that such a response is possible and forthcoming when I least expect it.

The impact of Christianity did not end, here, of course, and I continued to learn of theologians and people involved in the Clinical Pastoral Education movement who faced depression themselves. Interestingly, while this removed some of my disappointment in Christianity as a belief system, it did not remove the guilt, shame, and pretense I felt about my own story. So, it is Christianity, both in negative and positive ways, that permeated all my spirituality and affected most of my spiritual practices until this most recent decade of my life. I paid a heavy price for expanding my understanding of spirituality beyond Christianity even though none of those theologies, cosmologies, or systems of belief were anti-Christian at all. The personal, professional, and spiritual cost of those changes, however, contributed greatly to my final collapse.

Chronologically, traditional Christianity encompasses the largest portion of my life and it is the foundation of the ongoing evolution of my spirituality. I do not regret the inter-weavings of all kinds of Christianity throughout my story; nor do I regret finding a way out of those thoughts and beliefs that held me captive to a faith that, for the most part, did not contribute to my healing. It is part of the journey that led me to here, to the knowledge that it did not free me or my spirit. That experience allowed me to recognize those belief systems that did; and, for that, I am grateful.

It would be cumbersome to describe each part of my life in terms of spiraling and spinning; each of these events and the spiritual impact represent two inter-dependent life journeys descending and ascending at the same time. As I picture my life as two intersecting spirals, I see the many times that the melding of these spirals represents the place where my spiritual growth, pain and transformation live. Nevertheless, my story is complicated and complex—I have tried as best I can to draw some conclusions regarding the connections, although they are not perfect. I have found that, as convenient as it might be, the connections do not necessarily align and are not, as one would expect, precisely congruent. They are, however, part of the swirling, spinning spirals which encompass the 63 years of my life prior to my diagnosis.

The First Thirty Years or So: Beginning the Web

I was always a moody child, dark in thoughts and fearful of a great many things. Years later I learned that at an early age I was the subject of various kinds of abuse at the hands of my father, and that abuse, and mis-treatment caused aspects of my brain to begin to mis-fire. My father, too, experienced depression and unpredictable rages, but no one seemed to notice except my mother who was often the recipient of his seemingly unquenchable need to denigrate and mis-treat her. He was sexually, physically, and emotionally abusive to me as well. I lived in constant terror and learned to take pleasure outside the house with our collie dog, Holly, who I regarded as my safety net. When a school bus driver killed her before I turned six, I was bereft. Through all these years, my initial grounding in traditional religion began. However, my salvation during this time was not in the country church we attended; but, rather the hordes of cousins and my grand-parents with whom I spent my days.

Even at the early age of 5 and 6, my mind was on fire with questions about fairness and how a so-called loving God would allow such terrible things to happen to me. So began, even then, my quest to understand the parts of religion my young mind could not understand. It was also during these days; however, that I began to interact with nature in the backyard behind our four-room home. My twin sister was a robust child; I was not, and so I had plenty of time to take quiet refuge in nature and the hidden spirituality of nature and all the spirits inherent in trees, flowers, and every aspect of the natural world. I remember fondly making friends with nature and the supernatural during my difficult childhood. I became well acquainted with the fairies and sprites who lived under the white flowers at the base of the hill behind our house though I wouldn't have known what to call them.

But those playtimes were planted deep in my unconscious and they would resurface decades later. I also talked to trees and to the rocks that lined the creek that wound through our yard. I remember feeling that the safest place I could be was leaning up against a big tree and there were plenty from which to choose. I never tired of watching the limbs sway causing the leaves to lull me to a feeling of peace and rest. I suppose one could say my belief that everything was alive and had a soul began when I was three. Of course, I learned to reason my way out of these special relationships I explored as a young child; and, as most children do, went on to experience life in much the same way as the adults around me did, leaving behind my fairies, and loving and caring trees.

I was never a well child—all kinds of breathing problems plagued my early childhood. I had many bouts of pneumonia, bronchitis, and asthma. My inability to breathe received all kinds of medical explanations. I now believe it was certainly exacerbated, if not caused, by my feeling that I was holding my breath all the time—waiting for the next outburst or attack. Somewhere between the ages of 2 and 3, my hair fell out. Years later I discovered in my baby book that my mother had recorded that the doctor had suggested some trauma had caused this to happen. It does not appear that anyone ever sought to find out what that trauma was. Decades later, through flashbacks and years of therapy, the source of the trauma became evident.

On a spiritual level, I remember feeling quite abandoned, as if no one cared enough to make it stop. As a battered woman, my mother could do little to make it cease, but my fragile heart believed God was certainly doing nothing to stop it either. This did not coincide with the picture of God they showed in Sunday School. God could part the Red Sea but couldn't or wouldn't protect me from my father.

We also moved to Florida when I was 7. This meant leaving behind my grandparents, aunts and uncles and countless cousins with whom I had grown up thus far. My family told everyone, including me, we moved from Indiana to Florida because of my health. I bore the burden of this primal disruption until my mother finally told me when I was 16, that we had mostly gone to Florida to escape my father's creditors and move away from his constant indiscretions. When I was 10, my mother asked the pastor of the church we attended to support her as she explained that she and my father were divorcing. I could not have been happier had it not been for the obvious pain of my mother and sister.

During a 'last vacation' just before the divorce was final my father told me "I made him want to do 'bad' things to me." I lived with the ramifications of that declaration for decades. Experiencing abuse at the hands of a parent is a profoundly spiritual crisis. And when that same parent lays the guilt and shame of that abuse on your shoulders, it can take a lifetime to realize the impact on your heart. My heart, at age 10, was simply broken. Not only was I hurt, I was responsible. The fact that God had deserted me now made perfect sense to a confused 10-year-old mind. Why would God protect a child from something she brought on herself? While I had not yet experienced my first horrifying bout of depression, my father's frightening and disgusting remark laid the groundwork for later suffering. At the same time, I lived a double life. I continued to attend the church and Sunday School my mother attended but it did not contribute to my grasping for insight.

I was in the sixth grade the first time I was asked to leave a Sunday School class because I was upsetting the rest of the class with my impertinent questions. I learned quickly not to ask questions and I grew increasingly dissatisfied with the childish explanations of stories that simply had no relationship to my life. The fact that these Sunday School stories brought me no comfort at all was more than I could handle. I turned my questioning into doubt and my doubt into guilt. As I continued to try to make the stories make sense my doubt began to deepen. My participation in church activities continued because that is what we 'did' in my family and as a teenager those activities became increasingly significant as one of my primary social activities.

As described earlier, my first serious episode of depression and mania came when I was 17 years old and a junior in high school. Already addicted to Valium and Librium because I was depressed and the family doctor in a small town really did not know what else to do, I made every attempt to get myself to school. Much of the time, I didn't. As I said earlier, I sat cross-legged on my bed crying and screaming "God, what is wrong with me?" I was seriously suicidal and was acting out through a staunch and effective refusal to eat. I weighed 69 pounds and was slowly dying from Anorexia at about the same pace as

Karen Carpenter. Finally hospitalized, I made my escape by promising that I would keep my weight at 80 pounds or face hospitalization again. There were a lot of chocolate milkshakes in my life. The official diagnosis at the time was Neurocirculatory Asthenia. Now none of the symptoms associated with this syndrome fit what I was experiencing, but I suppose they had to tell my mother something. I was completely socially inept, painfully shy, and terrified of any group situation that required me to talk even though I forced myself to do it.

And every day, I heard more messages about who I should be in school and in my social community. Even though I was just barely able to find the tiniest voice of my inner self, I instinctively began to know there was significant dissonance between those messages and who I believed I was and wanted to be on my own terms. While I knew I was beginning to be molded into a person that did not resonate with the person I was secretly beginning to know, the other voices grew louder, and I learned to suppress any notion that those voices might be wrong. I began, on an increasingly painful level to loan more and more of myself to those who thought they knew what my life should look like. Like many with mental illness, I simply did not know how to find the strength or self-reliance to fight to reclaim those early glimpses of who I believed I was--spiritually or otherwise.

Although, it may seem completely out of place at this point in my story, I began to feel a call to become a 'healer'. Somehow, I knew that my eventual role on earth would be in some sort of healing activities. I answered that call in my deepest of hearts, although I had absolutely no idea what it meant or how I would reach that point in my life. I suppose I simply trusted that I would either reach it or I would not. Not long after, I began to speak of a call to 'ministry' of some sort. Somehow, I knew that this description would be far more acceptable than what I actually experienced in that 'call', but I had neither the vocabulary nor the guidance to begin to look at what my heart was telling me. The words with which I was familiar at that time simply failed my inner experience.

From my early teenage years until the years after seminary, the only thing other than Christianity I used to look for meaning were 'self-help' books. I always felt different from others and the constant depression didn't feel 'right'. I saw others get sad, but they always seemed to bounce back. I never did. I was, indeed, addicted to these self-help books. I was, as the saying goes, "the last book I read". I still remember my first foray into those kinds of books—*Psycho-Cybernetics* by Maxwell Maltz.[3] I poured over that book, looking for the secret formula to escape the constant darkness I experienced and become what I thought would be a fully functional (and maybe even happy) person. I would try new techniques, new ways of thinking or so I thought, positive thinking and affirmations and whatever else I was reading about. I followed the 'steps to happiness, change, whatever' with religious zeal. These books though interesting were ultimately useless in understanding the nature of my 'disease'. While not spiritual per se, I credit these books with keeping my hope in myself alive; and, in doing so, keeping me alive. There was, after all, an endless supply of self-help books out there and I talked myself into believing I just hadn't found the right one yet.

My church activities were many and varied. I was a leader in the youth group and began my gospel singing 'career' by traveling to local churches to hold concerts. I can say now, that I always, yes always, felt like a fraud, not because of my singing and speaking about a relationship with Jesus Christ but because it never really worked for me. This does not mean, of course, that it is not a truly valid expression of faith;

but it was not helpful in my fight against the grave depression through which I was wading. Throughout my late high school and college years I would 're-dedicate' my life to Jesus many times thinking that one of those times it would stick. So, even my extremely active church life brought with it a sense of hopelessness because what I shared with others through words and music was simply never true for me. It made me feel no better about who I was or why I was here. This was the first time I made a link between my depression and spirituality in my fragile mind. At the time, I would have used the words 'religion' or 'faith'. While my understanding of this was tenuous at best, the thoughts had begun to make themselves known amid my constant depression, anxiety, and lack of belief that I would ever truly be 'good' at anything. Additionally, this lack of faith in myself and all I was singing and saying called into question the faith of all those who 'seemed' to believe I had something to offer the world. They could not possibly be right, and I questioned why they were so easily 'conned' by me.

I was, quite simply, always depressed. I do not remember a time when anxiety and depression did not rule my life. Now there were times when I felt energetic, getting many things done at once, working hours upon hours in high school on prom dresses or staying up all hours of the night practicing as a music student in college. I now understand that this was a form of mania associated with Bipolar 2 Disorder. But the depression was always there, lurking behind every rock or tree I encountered. Interestingly enough, I loved to perform (although I did experience 'stage fright') and taking on the characteristics of whatever I was singing seemed to bring me relief from the depression I was battling. After nearly dropping out of college due to finances, my mother found the way to enable me to finish my last semester and I went on to become a music teacher for a couple of years. I did not feel fulfilled by what I was doing; and, again, waited for someone to tell me I was incapable of teaching little children to enjoy music or any other project I undertook at the time.

During my college years I made what I now consider a frightening venture into even more radical Christianity. Because I was a music student majoring in voice I was employed as a soloist in a church near the college. That church and the church in which I was involved at home had many members who were involved in the Neo-Charismatic Movement. I was ripe for the picking. Here, among Charismatics, the insistence on faith in Jesus' ability to heal was a significant aspect of the belief system. In my case, I tried deliverance of all manor of demon possession thinking that eventually we would happen on the right one. I was even able to identify that depression had a hold on me, but so-called deliverance from the demon of depression simply did not work. After numerous attempts at deliverance the depression remained. My anxiety worsened and some of the deliverance sessions I witnessed caused episodes of PTSD from incidents that terrified me from my childhood. I was a lost cause. I also saw others experiencing deliverance from their ailments and it seemed I was the only one for whom it did not work. I'm sure that was not true but in my troubled mind, it was very much a reality. This became particularly clear to me when after I experienced a sexual assault by a fellow student. I visited with a leader of the group who promptly decided that a deliverance session was in order. This 'session' turned out to be particularly alienating and disorienting. My existing pain and despair because of the assault became more intense by the so-called 'healing' attempts of the 'minister'. I felt guilty and ashamed. Eventually, I left that movement when my disillusionment and discomfort around the subjugation of women caused me to give up on that 'pathway to perfection' as well.

Nevertheless, during that same time I experienced the caring of a different social circle who did not take part in such activities and included other young adults and two wonderful adult mentors (our Sunday School Teachers). This circle of friends gave me some feeling of normalcy and belonging. However, my participation in both groups at once led to some difficulties for me and taught me even more about compartmentalizing the various aspects of my life, both psychically and spiritually.

I had an inner voice that called me, but I was unable, at this point in my life to hear the whisper of possible next steps to a different understanding of spirituality. I did not or was not able to follow my inner leadings; and, so for the next decade I gave away my spiritual power, did not seek a different way to experience transcendence; and, instead continued to look for ways to satisfy my longing for something more within acceptable norms or conventional thought. To be fair to myself, I grew up in a mostly conservative area of Central Florida, so I had no exposure to any alternative belief systems.

I made a return to more mainline, though conservative, religion and went to an almost all-male seminary. Again, depression prevailed, lessened only by the fact that the academic work was not particularly a challenge and I excelled even when it meant the derision of many of the male students. It was a hard life, however, being one of 30 women in an institution of 1200 men who were not happy, watching women challenge their superiority in all things spiritual and intellectual as they invaded a bastion of male religious segregation. Spiritually, I continued to seek comfort in those things which seemed to bring others great comfort and peace and, I simply failed.

Not surprisingly, I married before my last year of seminary and within weeks of my marriage entered one of the many 'black holes' of my life. It was not my new husband's fault; it just happened. I wouldn't come out of the bedroom (we must have been on winter break) except to watch the first airing of the mini-series of "Roots". Other than wanting to die, this is all I remember of these days.

After graduating, my husband and I moved to Austin, TX. While I loved the country-side and still find it one of the most exquisite places I ever lived, I was miserable. To top it off, I was doing an internship in Clinical Pastoral Education at the Austin State Mental Hospital. Even I somehow knew the irony in that. About a year after we moved to Austin, I found myself pregnant. Now, it was not a complete surprise; however, suffice it to say we thought it would take several years for this miracle to occur since I was diagnosed with many hormonal deficiencies because of my earlier anorexia.

My ordination in a moderately liberal Southern Baptist Church occurred at the beginning of my pregnancy. Again, religion, though not necessarily faith, played an important part in my life and I was thrilled to be one of the women ordained by a Southern Baptist Church which had only recently begun ordaining women in any considerable number. Because of my anxiety over my worthiness I was especially affected by the comments of insensitive ministers and deacons who were more concerned about whether I would put my husband's ministry first or try to make trouble for him. As a footnote, it is important to observe that I never worked full-time as a minister in the Southern Baptist Convention and, as previously noted, nearly lost my ordination in 1982. Although the denomination decided to rescind the ordinations of many of the women whom they ordained, a series of fortunate circumstances enabled me to retain my ordination. However, until much later in life and a change in denomination, I never worked more than part-time in any church and that work was mostly in music ministry.

I never truly recovered from the disillusionment that grew out of my increasing understanding that all I had worked for and thought I believed in truly had no meaning for anyone beyond myself. My husband's willingness to go along with the demeaning of my ordination to get a job for himself (even though we agreed I would do so) threw me into a period of existential doubt about my own worthiness and whether I ever wanted to be involved in such a system of beliefs. My heart and spirit were broken again; and the hypocrisy rampant in the evangelical denomination that had first ordained me and now wanted to deny my presence forced me to look at the interlocking aspects of those 'facts' on my depression. I felt powerless, discarded, and rejected.

Unfortunately, pregnancy was not an easy time for me. The glow never came, and I was sick right up to the night before my beautiful son was born. He was amazing, and I was thrilled; however, he was a colicky baby, had many ear infections and had his first bout with asthma when he was only a few months old. I did not get much sleep during those early years. Depression (probably post-partum) was overwhelming, I had no idea how to parent during the depression and made most of my decisions about how to do so based on the parenting I observed in the supposedly perfect families I saw on TV. My son's father was a good dad and I will always be grateful for the kind of parent he was. We moved to Florida where I tried to be a good mom and a good pastor's wife. I felt as if I was failing at both and depression deepened.

By the time, my son was three we had moved to Louisville, KY (again leaving my support system and my mother—this time in Florida)—so my husband could work on an advanced degree. For me, the depression worsened and made it almost impossible to parent or work. I was dismissed from a hospital chaplaincy program because my depression and anxiety were so clear to the supervisor that he did not want me in his program. As for parenting, it is not that I was abusive to this wonderful child; I just never really knew the best way to be the mom I wanted to be, and I was terrified of doing the wrong thing, and perhaps causing irreparable harm to my growing son.

My constant doubting of my ability to be a mother was at the heart of my feelings of immense failure. It is the root of one of my most significant spiritual 'woundings'. I truly did not know how to incorporate my feelings of failure into any spiritual understanding of the meaning of motherhood. Constant reading of spiritual books on parenting, womanhood, and, even self-care caused the depression to worsen. I never doubted that my son was a miracle. I just didn't know how to receive such a miracle amid primal doubt and guilt over unmet expectations about my capabilities.

When my son was three, I left the house, went to the home of a friend, and stayed three weeks. I couldn't be around my husband and didn't trust myself to parent my son. My mother eventually convinced me that I had to go back to avoid the accusation of abandonment. I later viewed this period as one of my major and most dangerous 'episodes'. Fortunately, I fell in the snow while I was there, bruised my tailbone and was prescribed pain pills. Their numbing effect probably saved my life. Nevertheless, it was clear to me the marriage was over, and I had to begin to do something about it. I began the painful process of separation and divorce. 'Shared custody' was popular at the time; and, it was the only thing to which my son's father would agree.

Briefly described, this meant my son had two day-cares, two bed-rooms, two sets of little friends and traveled back and forth between his parents every two weeks. (By this time, we lived about 80 miles apart because I had entered a Masters' program at Indiana University in Bloomington to reconnect with my extended family who still lived there.) The 'exchanges' when he had to return to his father were heart-wrenching for me. Although I now understand that children often have wonderful ways of making their parents feel unbearable guilt, I also know it was extremely painful for him to leave me. Every other week, his father would peel him off me and strap him, kicking and screaming, into his car seat, and I would drive the 32 miles home in absolute hysteria. No one understood. Literally, no one. I had one younger cousin (who may not even remember this) who used to make the trip with me when she could out of compassion for my sadness.

It was during this same time I began to face the inner knowledge that I was gay and simply did not know what to do with that except accumulate more guilt for failing my family and my God again. I would not act on these feelings for another few years, but the reality had finally hit, and things would never be the same again.

5

The Second Thirty Years and More: Enlarging the Web

As I briefly mentioned in the previous section, I had begun work on a second Masters' Degree. My work at Indiana University was fulfilling. However, I believe it was primarily a way to escape all the spiritual and existential questions that were haunting my life during this turbulent time. Because it was a generalized master's degree in Religious Studies, I had no choice but to look at other ways of thinking theologically. Although it certainly was not a logical choice for the administration to make, I was acting as an Assistant to the Professor of Eastern Religions (Buddhism, Taoism and Hinduism). I had no idea what I was doing and tried to stay a few pages ahead of the undergraduate students who were taking their mandatory writing course in that subject under my tutelage. My theological and spiritual life found new expression. I loved Taoist teachings and found myself in new territory including Buddhism that I enjoyed very much indeed.

Of course, it was frightening at first and I felt out of my element. Nevertheless, I persisted in this study and all it caused me to think about. I believe that my supervising professor observed two things about me: one, I was terribly, horribly, depressed all the time and she lovingly opened her door when I needed to cry; and, two, I was fascinated with the Eastern way of thought. She continued to encourage me to study those traditions even after I graduated and went on to doctoral studies. Probably because they served her so well, she suspected it might become valuable to me later in my life. Her welcoming spirit laid the groundwork for my return to Eastern traditions when I very much needed it.

My fascination with Buddhism, Taoism and Zen Meditation began during this time, but, in all honesty, I did not comprehend enough of the real principles of these systems of belief to have more than a cursory understanding of all that was involved. Years later, at least for a short period of time, I grew interested in Yoga and in Mindfulness Meditation both of which are grounded in Eastern traditions; and, I truly believe had Spirit not stepped in and caused me to be assigned, against all logic, to this particular professor and subject matter, I may never have been open to further exploration later on my spiritual journey.

In addition to all the general classes I took, the most important aspect of my work at Indiana University was my thesis which focused on the role of women in 19th Century Christianity in America. I was fascinated with the subject and studied primarily in the historical writings that linked Christian virtue for women to staying in the home, raising the next generation of men to be strong and to adhere to Christian values and girls to be 'good Christian wives' to those same strong men. My intellectual feminism (though not necessarily spiritual at this point) was birthed in this work and continued throughout my future work.

Even before I finished my degree at Indiana University, I received a fellowship for a doctoral program in New York City and began to study with some of the leading feminist scholars of the day. I'm sure it was an enjoyable time in my life although I was completely self-medicated on pain pills and valium. I tended to wash them down with White Zin. Since drugstores did not have today's sophisticated tracking systems, I was able to get any medication I wanted. Life was hard as a doctoral student. I had extraordinarily little money; and, not surprisingly, I eventually ran out of funds and never finished my Ph. D. This was an issue of great shame for me, but I really had no choice.

Stimulated academically, I enjoyed interacting with some of the Christian feminists who were making waves in the traditional Church. Feminism, profoundly influential in society, academia, and religion, also gave me the excuse I needed to stop struggling to feel I belonged. Many of these feminists tried to transform expressions of traditional religion with their amazing acts of courage and radical change, but I sat on the sidelines of those activities, feeling neither the passion nor the energy for that work. My overwhelming depression deprived me of any enthusiasm for working for change. I kept trying to grasp some sense of belonging to Christian churches; but, now, the misogyny that had been exposed and rejected by many of these women confused me even further. I was isolated and bewildered and had no idea what to 'do' with the religion of my childhood and young adulthood.

I did not take my son with me to New York City although he did spend most of the summers. Although, I was constantly depressed, I did the best I could to show him the sights of New York City. I never allowed myself to get high or have too much to drink when my son was in New York. I sobbed for days every August after I put him on a plane to send him back to his father. I knew it was for his own good; and I made occasional trips to see him during the year, but this period was a black hole of despair emotionally, mentally, and spiritually in my life. My family did not and could not understand how any mother could 'do this'—that is, give up her child. There was never any understanding I was making the best decision for my son I could make at the time.

When I took part in an 'intervention' for one of my professors who clearly had a problem with alcohol, I recognized myself in much that we said. I made the decision to get sober and stop self-medicating with pills. And I did. I did all the right things, 90 meetings in 90 days, in-patient rehab and finding a sponsor. And, for once in my life, something worked. I had a good sponsor initially and friends that supported my journey, and one of my proudest accomplishments is that I never relapsed or self-medicated in any way again. The anxiety and mental instability of early recovery was palatable.

I never experienced the spiritual side of recovery, did not really develop any community in 'the rooms' and did not utilize the 'program' to stay sober. I approached sobriety the same way I approached everything else—that is, I only had myself to rely on. I never really felt that sobriety was a spiritual process. I understand that, for most people in recovery it is a spiritual process, but it simply wasn't true for me. Physical and emotional practices (particularly learning to 'sit' with emotions rather than self-medicate) were obviously important; but I did not rely on a 'higher power' to somehow keep me sober. Such aspects of sobriety seemed to me to be psychological rather than spiritual.

Because I was committed to my sobriety and was not sure I could remain sober amid rampant opportunities to drink, smoke pot, and take pills, I went into in-patient rehab. Two friends were supportive of my decision to stay sober and they drove me the 100 miles or so to the rehab (which was in the middle of nowhere in upstate New York). Even though I had already been successfully sober for 40 days, I was terrified of what in-patient treatment would look like. Except for the food being even more inedible than I had imagined, there were no real surprises.

However, because I could not relate to the blatantly Christian emphasis on spirituality and its role in sobriety (at least in this center), I could not find a way to fit in here. The only time I felt the least bit in touch with Spirit was when I would walk down to the duck pond during our afternoon breaks. Here I could talk to the ducks, feel the breeze away from the stuffy stale air and begin to connect with something I knew to be bigger than I was. I didn't however give this source of peace any credit for my sobriety. I was engaging in alternative spirituality (particularly in the magic of Nature) even when I didn't know it. Mostly, I just felt out of place in a situation where I probably did not belong.

While there, I made what may have been one of the biggest mistakes of my life. I fell in love with one of the counselors; and, she saw a way to achieve her goal of finding someone to support her financially so that she did not need to work. She left the position with the rehab (or was fired) soon after we began spending a lot of time with each other (after I left the facility) and she made the decision to move to New York City. She moved in with me in my small studio apartment and stopped working. Little did I know she was a heroin addict who was, more than likely, not in recovery even when she was working as a counselor. I would stay with this woman for 11 years with one break where I tried to escape her manipulation and cruelty. My son came to live with us for one school year; and, all I knew was that I had to get him to safety. I couldn't save myself, but even though it broke both our hearts, he went back to live with his father. He would not live with me again until he was 19. I would see him, of course, but teen years took over slowly and he learned to live his life without his mother. I'm sure he did not understand that I was ill (since I did not understand this) but, somehow, he (and I) survived that prolonged period of rare visits and phone calls.

As for the practice of any form of religion or spirituality during most of those years, I simply did not. I was overwhelmed with self-hatred, fear regarding my survival, and intense feelings of unworthiness. Giving myself over to this woman left me in a state of constant crisis and despair. During this time, I was working in social services with abused children, their families, and foster families. I eventually moved to administration and became a trainer for the state of New York as well as continuing my job in social services. Professionally, it was rewarding; but it hit a little too close to home for me to be truly satisfied. I remember, at one point, thinking and saying that most of the abusive parents I saw had undiagnosed Bipolar Disorder; but, never made the connection to my own experience.

I lived a completely split existence. At work I was a strong capable woman. At home I was weak and afraid. I continued to stay with this woman who spent every penny I earned (much of it on drugs and gold jewelry) and I remained depressed beyond reason. During this time, while I was working full time and running retail businesses she wanted to start, I started to engage in self-harming behavior. I became a 'cutter' inflicting cuts on my lower arms. It was the only control I had, and the only way I had to relieve the stress I was enduring. It was extremely important that none of my supervisors or co-workers know of this behavior, so I wore long sleeve shirts and never, never asked for help. My partner was cruel and controlling. I was terrified of her and terrified to leave her. I'd like to blame my round the clock working on mania of some sort (and I'm sure it played a role); but, this time, it was pure un-adulterated fear that kept me up at night stocking the store that she wanted while working a full-time job during the day. Then, to make some money back, I would work on Saturday and Sunday keeping the store open as long as I could.

She insisted on having control over all monies: and, as a result, I had both a car repossessed and lost my driver's license because she chose not to pay the insurance on our remaining car which was titled in my name. I don't even remember how I got to work at that point. I was so exhausted and despairing that some of this time is simply missing. I had to go through the humiliating experience of asking my supervisor to sign for my work-only driving permit and beg her to allow me to continue to drive company cars as I did my home studies for foster parents. During this same time, this woman stayed at home, shooting up and having an affair with at least one client as she failed miserably as a therapist. I was suicidal. I tell you about her to illustrate again how unable I was to care for myself and save myself from predators. My father had taught me well; and, the on-going depression kept me prisoner. During this lengthy period of time spirituality played little, if any, role in my life. And, if I had wanted to engage in some spiritual practice or find a spiritual community, I simply had no time to waste on my soul.

Eventually, after eviction from both the store and the home where we lived occurred; I decided to leave her. I eventually moved into an acceptable apartment. I had no car, and so, was dependent on either a ride from friends to work or walking, sometimes through the snow and ice. I often walked the 45-minute commute home and I was full of shame and wanted to die. My walks home were marked with tears and thoughts of how to end the life I was living. I simply had no hope.

I felt completely deserted by God and by family. Spiritually, I was dead and had little hope of surviving.

My anxiety was overwhelming; and, it didn't take much for me to agree to live with her again (which really meant that I would continue to fund her unhealthy lifestyle and addictions). Around this time, I decided I would really have to give in and go to therapy. My first therapist was kind and encouraged me to leave my abuser a second time. Beyond that, she was not helpful, and I later found out she was battling her own demons of drug addiction at the time she was seeing me. During the 11 months this woman and I were back together, it was necessary for me to drive back and forth across a bridge that spanned the Hudson River to feed her exotic birds that I could not keep in my apartment. I made sure to take our dog with me, so I would not drive the car off the bridge. That dog saved my life.

At the same time, my best friend in New York, who is still a dear friend to this day, tried everything she knew to do but was unable to stop me from my destructive behavior. I was unable to see the depth of her concern and frustration. My family simply remained angry that I 'allowed' this woman to encourage me to be estranged from them and live such an unpredictable lifestyle.

Finally, I found a therapist who worked with me for 8 years. We worked through some of my 'abuse issues' and the need for me to leave this woman for a final time. I was able to buy a car for $500 and moved into the first place I had been happy in years. I had a sense of euphoria at first even though she insisted on showing up occasionally, one time giving me a Persian kitten as a way of maintaining some contact with me. But, for the most part, I was free and the flow of money to her ceased. I lived pay-check to pay-check, but I was out of the hell of the last 11 years.

Although this would certainly not be my last attempt at a relationship, every attempt left me deeper and deeper in despair. This sense of unworthiness played out in my spiritual life by my being convinced that not only did I not deserve a human relationship, I did not deserve a relationship with Spirit either. I believed that I was totally and utterly alone in my need to be loved and embraced. This would haunt my desire for a spiritual relationship with something (quite frankly, anything) bigger than me.

Not too long after this move, my then 19-year-old son needed to move in with me in New York. I welcomed the opportunity to rebuild a relationship with him; and because he is an amazing son, we were able to do that. My shame and guilt nearly overwhelmed me though; and, it was my incredibly wise son who begged me to stop punishing myself and just enjoy our new relationship. He lived with me through his college years and first year of work until he finally moved off to New York City where he was employed. These were some of my best years. My joy at having him back in my life and the opportunity to have a second chance to be his mother kept me mostly stable through those years.

I was also slowly rebuilding my relationship with my own family as well since my long relationship with the woman I spoke about above left me completely estranged from them. As is usual in abusive relationships, she had been controlling and demanding that I choose between her and my family. I made an unwise choice. Nevertheless, I often wondered later why someone in my family didn't see what was happening during the long dark years of the soul-killing relationship I had endured and try to save me. Their seeming lack of interest in my well-being was something I tried to come to terms with for years. What felt like their abandonment further increased my feelings of hopelessness. I knew I had hurt each of them in separate ways, but I naively believed they would somehow know I desperately needed saving from myself. Although I was long past being 'grown up' these feelings troubled me and left me feeling like the 5-year-old child who needed saving from her father.

During this time, I also enjoyed (or so I thought) a two-year relationship with a woman whom I adored. We fell into a satisfying relationship even though she was having difficulty separating from her ex-partner. Finally, the inevitable happened. She told me she had never really loved me, and that the relationship was over. Darkness over another broken relationship was heavy; but having my son in my life gave me meaning; and, slowly the failure of another relationship slipped into the category of 'normal' for me. I would be single for at least 5 years this time; and, I convinced myself I was using the time to 'work' on myself and figure out who I wanted for my next relationship. I was not yet 50 years old and had already had enough failed relationships to last a life time. It never occurred to me that I was making terrible choices because I was coming from a place of complete terror about being 'alone' and fear that all these failed relationships in my life confirmed my ultimate unworthiness of deserving a happy life.

Having my son live with me brought a certain sense of normalcy to my life. Because he had asked repeatedly, I attended the Episcopal Church he was attending and became active. I sang in the choir and even preached a time or two. I felt welcome. I even considered becoming a priest as the pull toward fulfilling my long ago calling seemed reasonable at the time. The financial requirements and inability to quit my job kept me from pursuing it; but, once again faith seemed to be taking hold after years of exile from organized religion. I think it was the pomp and ritual in the Episcopal Church that appealed to me spiritually. I was 'hiding in plain sight' in all that was going on and it was never necessary to talk about what I really believed. It was an easy place to disappear.

I was financially secure, or so I thought, working three jobs at times because I had energy and wanted to be creative. I was traveling (using vacation and personal days from my actual job) throughout New York State presenting trainings I had created in my consulting job. This, for some reason, re-awakened my feelings of being 'found out'; that is, not the respected trainer I appeared to be. I kept at it, but it brought with it a sense of foreboding that all was not well. Looking back (and this may have been the source of the confused and defeatist thinking), I realize that this was a time of extreme mania causing me to think I could do anything on little sleep or leisure time. Even though I was making good money, I couldn't seem to stop spending it and so had truly little extra to fall back on. I was still seeing the same therapist and we went through several diagnoses, mostly landing on clinical depression, PTSD, and panic disorder. She even briefly considered a diagnosis of Dissociative Identity Disorder since I tended to show up one week extremely depressed and the next week euphoric about something or another. I even tried to confirm that diagnosis by sending her 'letters' from various 'parts' of my disintegrated self. I would have done anything to know what was 'wrong with me'.

Depression was still more prevalent than euphoria and I suppose that Bipolar or any mood disorder did not occur to her since I was a functioning professional woman. It would take another 16 years to get an accurate diagnosis. I was off and on anti-depressants for decades; sometimes they worked and most times they didn't. I saw several psychiatrists during this time as this was a requirement of my insurance and was the only way to get the anti-depressants or therapy. Quite frankly, each one seemed less competent than the next and so it does not surprise me that no correct diagnosis ever happened. So, despite what looked like progress, I was profoundly depressed, and anxiety was beginning to become a larger part of my life. I was alone and had been so for several years. I was convinced my life circumstances would not change. This was destructive in several differing ways. For one thing I believed I would always have the kind of money I currently had and so I spent into the future, not realizing I would someday be unable to pay off those debts. Secondly, my belief I would always be alone and my despair about that kept me from enjoying the life I had. I tried; I really did; but joy was far away.

After my son moved out on his own, my animals began to take on life-preserving significance even though I had a social life and a few close friends. I discovered again that, just as in my childhood, my animals saved my life. My dog Jonathan and my cat Solomon (and my son's cat off and on) kept me alive. Many, if not most, Saturday mornings, Jonathan and I would get up and drive into the Berkshire Mountains; or all the way to Vermont. This time spent with my traveler dog gave meaning to my life during these years. I was passionately devoted to him and him to me. He encouraged me (as only dogs can) to get up each morning and start again.

Even then I was beginning to re-establish the priority of nature in my life and experienced much peace in the forests through which I sojourned. As I look back on it, this re-uniting with the nature of my childhood began the long journey into alternative spirituality which eventually led (many years later) to a completely new understanding of the Sacred long before I understood the spiritual needs of my fragile and un-focused mind. Fatigue was unrelenting, but I always found the energy to get myself out into nature since, on some level, I must have known it was saving my life. Nature, and hiking through the woods, began to take on new meaning and I spent as much time as possible exploring every trail and park in the area with my intrepid 16-pound Jonathan in the lead.

I began to see seeds of new ways of thinking about spirituality—and found the freedom to move away from earlier traditions into yoga and mindfulness. I had an amazing chiropractor who introduced me to Reiki, Healing Touch, and other forms of energy healing. It was wonderful and kept me going. For the first time in many years, life settled into a boring sameness with few changes. I was beginning to suspect that there might be something more 'out there' for me to explore. I lived near Woodstock, NY, and had plenty of opportunity to choose service providers who believed in and practiced alternative healing. I sought them out as well as engaging in yoga for a few years and took classes in mindfulness meditation. I began my study in Reiki reaching Level 2; but did not continue as life became complicated again. Upon reflection, I believe deep inside me, I knew I had begun to spiral down into a place of extreme depression that was the beginning of a long journey to the end. I must have been around 45. After 30+ years of living with an undiagnosed mental illness, the depression and anxiety were beginning to take its toll. But, 15+ years would pass before it overtook me, and I finally received a diagnosis.

Spiritually, I was still seeking a way to fully experience the transcendence I knew was OUT there (it didn't occur to me I was looking outward instead of inward). I also, on a very real level, began, ever so slowly, to believe that my depression and anxiety were, indeed, linked to this search. I remember as I was studying yoga and meditation that I hoped I would be able to make a meaningful connection between my spirit and my mind. It is not that I didn't, I just couldn't seem to make it last between the episodes of depression and mania.

In my next job, I was living in a small town in Eastern New York completely isolated from my earlier support system. I was again attending an Episcopal church but my enthusiasm for organized religion was becoming less and less. I found it impossible to confide the depths of my struggle to the kind and compassionate priest; although, I believe he had an inkling of my despair and tried to befriend me. In this job, my boss and I tangled from the beginning. It was freezing cold; and I made so little money that year I could not pay for enough heating oil so the home I lived in stayed at 50 degrees at night and I cried myself to sleep every night because I was so cold. I never asked for help. To admit defeat at this stage of my life was something I just couldn't do. I was in trouble financially, trying to make credit card payments I had taken on when I was making decent money (which I wrongly thought would never end) and barely making it. I felt alone and unlovable. I seemed, or so I thought, to struggle through every episode in my life completely alone.

I had several friends during this brief stay in this small town, including one special relationship with a woman who remains my friend to this day. Being able to talk to her (she was engaged in academic pursuits at the time) enabled me to reconnect with diverse ways of thinking and her friendship was crucial to living through the negative job situation and extreme loneliness at the time. However, with regard to romantic relationships, I came to realize that I often engaged in relationships that were headed for disaster before they started. I was proving on a physical and emotional plane what I believed about my inability to have a relationship with the Sacred. I was still a long way from giving myself permission to seek new ways and new thoughts.

I was working my occasional consulting job in addition to my full-time position, but it was a challenging time. Money for training in non-profits decreased and those opportunities came with less and less frequency (not just for me, but for all of us who were 'moonlighting' as trainers). As this was my only other avenue for additional funds my financial situation continued to deteriorate. My depression and anxiety made it almost impossible to do my job; and, eventually, I knew I was going to lose it due to disagreements with my boss. I was falling into the abyss again. I was slowly coming to the knowledge that I was about to be unemployed in a town of 900 people; and, even though it was now almost spring, the thoughts of another winter were unbearable.

As Spring headed into Summer, I did something I had never done. I quit my job and moved to Florida where I would be close to my now aging mother. While I was happy to be leaving both the job and the Northeast (although I was leaving my son in New York City) I was, nevertheless, horribly depressed, and anxious about finding work and being utterly and completely alone. I, of course, did not seek help at this time, finally believing this would be the nature of my emotional life and that trying to change was simply a pipe dream. This change and the upheaval it brought to my life caused me to simply give up. I filled what little spare time I had by reading sometimes 6 or 7 light mysteries in a week to keep my mind occupied.

At first, I did not look for any spiritual outlet for myself as I was taking my mother to her Presbyterian Church and beyond singing in their choir, my spiritual life was in hiding from me. I found myself turning to nature and made treks to sacred places I had discovered decades ago—the beach, an ancient cemetery in St. Augustine, and a park in Winter Park that had been a 'decision-making place' for me since I was in college.

Jonathan and I now traveled often to places I had visited as a child and adolescent trying to reconnect with my return 'home'. I had not lived in Florida for decades. I remember sitting on a bench in the St. Augustine cemetery looking out over the bay with Jonathan beside me. I cried, asking for someone, anyone, to give me a sign that I had made the right decision to return to Florida. The silence was deafening, and I left there bereft and thinking once again of suicide and defeat. Again, I had no overt spiritual experience that kept me alive, but I would not allow my mother to think I had committed suicide because I had come to Florida to care for her. In retrospect, I realize that this was indeed Spirit using whatever it took to keep me alive long enough for me to see my own self-worth and to experience the unconditional love of the Universe. Spirit is patient and trustworthy although it would take me many more years to fully understand.

Almost at once, I took a job in an agency working with abused children and supervising a team of young caseworkers. I was too afraid of ending up unemployed long term to say 'no' to this job offer. I hated every minute of this job. Though I only rarely considered returning to New York, I did not know how to make this life-altering move work. Depressed and alone, Jonathan and my cat, Solomon, were sometimes my only source of comfort. I did not seek therapy at this time, or even medical help as it all seemed too hopeless to try. My mother and step-father loved having me around though, so I spent a lot of time taking them to dinner and shopping for them. In some ways it was a relief to have someone who needed me. It gave me a sense of purpose at least.

In despair and loneliness, I had a very brief fling with a woman I met online and made almost immediate plans to move some four hours south of my mother to be with this woman. I had switched from depression to mania and was not making any decisions that made sense to anyone who knew me. I only hoped such a move and relationship would alleviate my daily despair. That move would have invalidated my plan to care for my mother and would have required my giving up my treasured dog, Jonathan, who had been my companion for years. Nevertheless, I was remarkably close to looking for work there when she suddenly decided she did not want to continue with these plans. She announced this to me on my last four-hour trip on the Florida Turnpike; and, while I was devastated, I soon realized that she had, in fact, kept me from a poorly thought-out, heart-breaking decision. Although I know I hurt my mother in my willingness to move after being in Florida less than two years and her increasing need for my presence, she did not try to stop me from planning to do it. I think that she may have been more upset over the thought that I would part with Jonathan than with my leaving Central Florida where she lived.

After months of juggling a job that was unpredictable in hours, taking care of my mother and transporting her to see my step-father who had moved to assisted living, I was close to collapse. I was holding it together, had a friend or two but, in the dark of the night, I struggled mightily with depression and anxiety. Again, I did not seek help because I was supposed to be the helper. I was clearly in a period of hypo-mania throughout most of this time, pushing myself beyond belief and living on adrenaline and the fear that if I slowed down or stopped what I was doing, it would be all over. At some point during this period, I was involved in a moderately serious auto accident. I totaled my car, broke several ribs, and was badly bruised. Although the accident was not my fault, the resulting weeks of pain caused my anguish over my job and social isolation to escalate. I spent the few spare evenings I had in my apartment, and slowly walking Jonathan throughout the complex.

Eventually, and quite by accident, I found my way back to religion in a significant way. Metropolitan Community Churches is a denomination of churches that reaches out to LGBTQI people; and, while I knew of MCC, I had never lived close enough to one to attend regularly. I went to their webpage simply to find out service times and found that they were seeking a full-time minister of music with other pastoral duties. I applied for the job and got it. They accepted my earlier ordination and I began the work of transferring my credentials; and, while it was a significant cut in pay, it was a particularly good thing. Almost immediately, though, the feelings from my adolescence and young adulthood began to whisper ever so subtly in my ear and I struggled with depression and anxiety throughout most of this position. I never genuinely believed I was good enough to do this job and struggled with the notion that I was pretending again to be someone who I was not.

I never said anything or sang anything in this church I did not believe. But I believed it differently now. That did not keep me from singing praise songs or lifting my hands in gratitude. I imagine some in that church would think that I was dishonest during those years and I can understand why. Nevertheless, that was not the case. It's also true that I wanted desperately to believe with the same faith I saw in others, but I just could not. I felt 18 again and was singing and preaching things in ways that I believed people would want to hear them, never realizing the damage it was doing to my heart. It also never occurred to me until years later and another failed attempt at serving in a Christian church that I was also failing folks who, just like me, were looking for other ways to express and experience their beliefs. At the time, though, I could not see beyond my failure, my self-doubt, and my feelings of unworthiness.

I met a woman (who I love dearly to this day) and we had our first date around the 4th of July 2008. I moved in with her about a month later. After another month, she asked me to marry her. I said 'yes'. I will leave aside her impulsivity—that is for her to tell; what is important in my story is my inability to slow down my life long enough to say, "wait, this is too fast". I threw myself into ceremony preparations as marriage wasn't legal at that point, and in making sure I attended to my mother as well. She insisted on living alone and, even though I lived only about a mile from her at this point, it was difficult to balance job, new relationship, and ailing mother. I was frantic and depressed, and hiding it as well as I could.

One early morning, we received the call I had been dreading. My mother had fallen and needed us. One look at her and I called 911 with a sense of foreboding that this might be the beginning of the end. She spent months in a rehab waiting to recover to the point where she could have her hip replacement repaired. I was able to visit her at least six days a week; and when I couldn't, my partner did. She loved my partner dearly and I credit her with enabling my mother to finally accept that I was gay. My mother never expressed any displeasure again. She died before that relationship was over and I remain grateful that she saw a mutually loving relationship in contrast to all that had gone before.

After her surgery and additional rehab, she eventually agreed to live in assisted living; but did not handle the situation well. She chose to go into assisted living close to where my sister lived which was over an hour from where I lived, so I added Saturday trips to my already shaky schedule. Meanwhile, the ceremony was drawing closer and my new relationship had settled into a kind of normalcy despite all the distractions. My partner decided after a period of unemployment to become a long-distance truck driver. I was supportive even though I knew it might mean long separations for us. Underneath it all, the thoughts, "I didn't sign up for this" began to brew and send me headlong out of mania into dire depression.

She was due to leave on her first training trip the week after our 'honeymoon' and I could not seem to accept that she was going to leave. On the last night of our stay in Gatlinburg, I completely lost it--screaming and crying and unable to come to terms with any of what was happening to me. I honestly feared I was entering psychosis. I came completely apart, unable to even comprehend where I was or what was happening. Eventually I cried my way into darkness that would not lift for years.

There were no more periods of hypo-mania until after my mother died. My mother died a horrible death. Eventually, she was diagnosed with an extremely rare and virulent form of bone cancer. The pain was unbearable and the diagnosis months in coming. All this time, my mother refused to allow us to tell her the nature of her diagnosis. She was angry—mostly at God, but at us as well. When the hospital could not keep her comfortable, we moved her to Hospice under the guise of finding her a better place to live. She thought the placement in Hospice was temporary. I was numb and just hoping for her pain to end. My son came from New York to see his grandmother; and, while I think she knew she was telling him goodbye, she never admitted it to me. A little over six weeks after her diagnosis, the morphine coma set in and most, though not all her pain, was alleviated.

Before the coma took her mind, she did not ever want to know her diagnosis. She did not tell me that she was proud of me or that she loved me or thank me for all the care I had given to her during the last years. She simply said nothing except to rant at God for 'doing this to her'. This was a profound spiritual crisis for her; and, in turn, for me. My mother had always been a religious woman; and, for her faith to fail her at this point reopened all my previous doubts and confusion. Nevertheless, I was with her as she died, and she gave me one of the most incredible spiritual experiences of my life. She opened her eyes and smiled at me. In my mother's later years, she had gone almost completely blind; but I knew in that moment her sight had returned though, more than likely, focused on a world I could not see. I came to understand in that one moment that she was at peace; and, though she never took the chance to say it, I believed that she loved me with the deep love a mother has for her child.

Two months after her death, my partner and I began to make plans to move. I was invited to move to a wonderful place in North Central Florida and begin to plant what would later become a flourishing church. This church was a part of the inclusive denomination in which I was already working, and I was involved in an exciting new project. Particularly in the early years, I worked long hours and often felt like the man on the Ed Sullivan show—the one who kept many plates all spinning on poles at the same time. Just like him, I was running from pole to pole to keep the plates all spinning. I, too, was spinning out of control, trying to keep almost 100 people at any one time happy and comfortable with the church we were building together. Looking back, it is clear to me that I never even thought about giving myself time to grieve my mother's death. I took that sorrow into my 'new' life. Not only did I not grieve her death itself, I was unable to grieve my despair over my inability to alleviate her physical and spiritual pain during her transition process. It was as if I believed I was invincible to grief even though her death, the circumstances of her death and my own spiritual crisis around her death were adding extra weight to the overwhelming panic that was beginning to emerge.

I honestly believed that a fully authentic inclusive congregation would be able to make room, even welcome, people from other traditions, beliefs, or no beliefs at all. I was honest from the first time I met with this small group of people that this was my dream. Even the name of the church, 'Open Circle,' suggested a welcoming, inclusive place. And, I believe most of those who joined in this venture wanted the same. This church grew rapidly, receiving high regard as a new model for church planting throughout the denomination. However, I may have forgotten in my enthusiasm for inclusivism and diversity, that churches are not perfect and people (including the pastor) who are in churches are not perfect.

My own theology at the time was far from traditional and my sermons honestly reflected that. I had continued to evolve away from mainline Christianity into a more expansive view of God, the Universe and spirituality. I led the music for much of the time in this church and was experiencing another shift in my interpretation of 'church music'. At least in the praise and worship songs, I could understand them in the context of the Universe itself or some higher power. It seemed pointless and unnecessarily confusing to try to explain this to the congregation. I continued to lift my hands, but this time it was in praise to something higher than the generally accepted meaning of these songs. Some of this was unconscious at the time, but much of it was not. Whichever the case, I began to experience the split between my beliefs and the beliefs of many in the congregation. My regret throughout this period was that I believed I could not share my truth. Perhaps, my heart was beginning to recognize—if only dimly—the feelings that were beginning to surface in some of the congregation.

It began to be clear to me that the more traditional followers in the church I had founded were beginning to be increasingly uncomfortable. I tried, to the best of my ability, to walk both sides of the road at the same time. The stress was becoming unbearable, but my desire to keep this church growing won out and I continued to push myself more and more looking for things that might interest increasing numbers of people with varying viewpoints and priorities.

My physical health was suffering. I experienced a month-long bout with shingles. The physical pain of the shingles was almost a relief compared to the mental, emotional, and spiritual drama that was playing out in my heart all the time. I also returned to taking anti-depressants, which truly had no effect at all on the pain and turmoil I was experiencing. At some point in this time, my partner and I broke up and I found myself alone to struggle with my own inner darkness and profound loneliness. To her credit, she never stopped supporting me or the church and was a reliable source of strength at the time. After a few brief months for both of us to recover from the breakup, my ex-partner and I continued to be and still are good friends.

A few others also provided support and leadership especially one special couple who devoted hours to the running of the church. Not only was their friendship and support crucial during those years, they were to become vital to my survival when the end of my ability to cope at all finally occurred several years later. There were others who were supportive; but I increasingly began to have trouble differentiating between those who truly supported me as a person or me as their pastor and those who did not.

At some point during this time, I was in a very brief relationship with a woman I barely knew. Nevertheless, we bought a house together and I sold the house I had purchased several years before. She had needs and expectations that did not match mine and she soon came to believe I had a host of problems she could not tolerate. One terrible night we engaged in a yelling match that left me sobbing and begging her not to leave me. Again, psychosis seemed close, even in the moment, and I was afraid of losing my grip on reality. Because of my fear of being alone again I promised her anything she wanted. However, the next morning, she remained firm that the relationship had ended, and I gave up in despair and moved out. I was now just barely making it financially because I had to rent a home at a cost far more than my previous mortgage. I was using my small inheritance from my mother to stay afloat financially. I was beyond devastated, terribly embarrassed that, as the congregation's pastor I had already been in two relationships; and, I again believed that I should stay single forever. I was just past 60.

My resolve did not hold as I was desperately looking for relief from the constant psychic pain I was enduring from the loneliness and anxiety from all that was transpiring in the church I was working so hard to maintain. Six months later, I began a relationship with a woman with whom I thought I could build a lasting family. She was also supportive of my ministry in this church. At the same time, I lost my trusted dog, Jonathan, who had done so much to save my life throughout the hollow times. Three days later, I brought Finian into my life because I knew I had a dog-sized hole in my heart that was crucial for me to fill. Somewhere deep inside I knew, at times, it was my love for my dog and my dog's love for me that kept me alive. My little Fin became my constant companion and began his 'job' as my traveling dog and mood lifter.

As a pastor, I should probably have paid more attention to the discomfort of some of my parishioners; but, to be fair to myself, I was receiving far more positive than negative feedback about my sermons (almost all of which were inclusive of various traditions) and other programs I was integrating into the Church's activities. The dissent, unfortunately, remained hidden underground.

In July of 2013, I preached a sermon about diversity. I include these brief passages because they illustrate what I was hoping to bring to this faith community. "...theological differences are good—something to celebrate, cherish and seek. Honesty is honored as the necessary pre-requisite for spiritual formation and growth. ...Theological diversity is, in this case, far more than just rituals and rites. It is about opening our doors to people who describe God differently, experience God differently, and speak of God differently. In this loving embrace—free from fear and judgment. ...we must become the kind of community where people flock because they know judgment of one another is not tolerated, where open and loving arms are celebrated, where the hurts of the world are made bearable by the fellowship of all gathered together, and our spirits are bonded together in the knowledge that we are all loved and cherished."

Sermons can be inspiring, even life-changing; but only Spirit and the willingness of those who preach or hear can turn mere words into reality. My anxiety made it difficult for me to handle the conflict and my depression rendered me hopeless that change could occur. As the months continued, discord began to turn truly hurtful and it seemed I was powerless and unable to have any real effect on the climate of the church. All my insecurities surfaced; and I was suffocating from the collision of the fear of failing personally and professionally and being untrue to myself spiritually. My vocation or 'call' to ministry, the subtle feelings of loss that accompanied it, and my not so latent perfectionism was interwoven throughout my journey; and had been greatly informed by and has influenced my experience with mental illness.

My spirituality during this time was both at its strongest and weakest simultaneously. I had come into a spiritual power and was certain of what I believed. And I knew that I was about to pay a huge price for that knowledge and my unwillingness to deny my Truth. Everything exploded at once. I questioned everything I ever thought about my 'call' to vocational ministry. I questioned the years I had put into that call and re-examined my ability to serve and be faithful to myself at the same time.

Midway through the fourth year of my ministry with this church, a group of unhappy people surfaced and things in the church became simply unbearable for me and for many. I called for an intervention from the denomination, one of the only resources I had in hand; and, when that failed, I began to break down into deeper and deeper despair. The experiment of this new church did not end well for me and for many others. Sadly, the openness and inclusivity did not find welcome by a vocal minority of the congregants; and, I eventually retired from this church amid unrelenting pain, depression, confusion, and hopelessness. Although I had begun a new relationship several months prior to my retirement and there were a few loyal parishioners who wanted to push back against this insurgence, I felt utterly alone. I experienced unrelenting depression, anxiety, and thoughts of walking away from life altogether.

My evolving spirituality that had been so dear to me and my joy at finding a way to express it betrayed me at every point. I was desperate. It was too late to go back, nor did I want to. This experience of rejection, however, over the long haul, changed my view of myself and my self-acceptance and set the stage for the crisis that followed in the next year or so. Even when I found new avenues to express my spirituality, the pain of this rejection haunted me.

Somehow, I knew I had reached a breaking point and I announced my retirement from pastoral ministry and from this church. I remember the night the fire went out. The Board of Directors received the report from the denomination that was scheduled for presentation to the congregation the next day. Feeling betrayed and alone, I decided to move my retirement up by several months and sat with silent tears running down my face the entire meeting. The 'goodbyes' were mediocre from many and lukewarm from all but a few. Many told me of their love for me, but none (other than some Board members and a few people who had significant ministries within the church) had done anything to help heal this congregation and I knew my fragile mind and heart could no longer fight. Perhaps I should have known my inability to cope was nearing, but it did not fully come until almost a year later. My attempt at involvement in mainline Christianity simply stopped with the disillusionment of this failed endeavor and I began to resolutely search for the ability to speak powerfully of my truth that I had been struggling to speak for years.

And, yet, there was a spiritual freedom that went with this time of breakdown of what I thought were my dreams and calling. I was free to express that same calling in more authentic ways—ways that spoke of my Truth and who I experienced myself to be as a minister and healer. My spirit was free; but the road still stretched out in front of me. I was spiritually, emotionally, and physically exhausted. While I could celebrate this newly found 'freedom', I was not at all certain I was prepared or able at that time to move into my Truth. And, indeed, I wasn't. Immediately after leaving the church, I moved to Asheville, NC, with my then partner. At this point, I had known her for about

8 months. I, quite frankly, did not care where I ended up and thought Asheville was as good a place as any to escape the pain and disappointment that had overtaken my life. I learned later that Asheville is *a spiritual vortex* or a place where Spirit is particularly active. I found that to be true while I was there as even in my later despair, I felt a certain 'something' that I could only describe as a special presence. We moved to a cabin on a mountain with beautiful views and I hoped my healing would begin.

I found two sources of spirituality when I first moved to Asheville that gave me great hope and peace. I had gone to Asheville because my then partner asked me to; but, just as importantly, I had gone to escape the constant reminders of one of the most painful experiences of the last half of my life—the loss of a faith community to whom I had devoted my heart and soul. I wanted to run away and so I did. Whether or not I should have no longer matters; I did. Almost at once I began to attend a Quaker Meeting. The way they conducted church business was a balm to my hurting soul. They really did address each other as 'Friend' and they meant it. My weary heart and soul longed to know anew that people could disagree or agree and still be 'friends'. Whether valid or not, my spirit had been so damaged and my trust in my own spiritual nature had been so wounded, that this was the 'soul medicine' I needed.

This loving and tender group of people showed me a way that stayed with me throughout my darkest hours that were to come. I would return repeatedly to the memories of a faith community that, agree or not, placed the notion of friendship and community higher than individual interest or gain. In many ways they introduced me to the word 'tender' and it, literally, changed my perspective on the Divine, on community, and on myself and my own spiritual journey.

I felt cradled in the embrace of this community although as my life broke apart, I was certainly unable to tell them. Because of all they taught me and, I guess, to honor them in some way, I named my newly designed and published website 'The Tender Journey'. These loving kind people restored my spirit in so many ways--the sitting in silence, waiting for Spirit to speak was really all I could manage in those early days. But Spirit always spoke, and I kept the belief that Spirit was not dead to me nor I to Spirit.

A couple of months later, I began working for and attending a Unity Church. In a completely unique way, this community and their amazing minister contributed further to my return to believing in the validity of my own heart and the authenticity of my spiritual maturity. There I found joy and enthusiasm. I watched others as they experienced the joy that pervaded each service. And though I spent a lot of those services hiding my tears as my heart slowly began to re-open to that very joy, I was able to experience the possibility of light returning to my spirit. Unity churches also embrace all forms of spirituality and, for the first time, I experienced the feeling of being 'safe' in a faith community. I split my Sundays between these two communities and came to know balance and harmony in new and reassuring ways. But the peace that had emerged vanished in one unexpected moment as if a mirage.

Approximately five months after we moved to Asheville, my partner announced that neither Asheville nor I was what she wanted in her life and she returned to Florida rather quickly and I was left to pick up the pieces of an expensive move which had emptied my small savings account and added a personal loan, maxed out my credit card, and left me bereft of any significant local support. The minister with whom I worked was as supportive as she could be but, as she told me later, she did not know the depths of my despair. I simply could not bring myself to tell anyone how desperate my mental situation truly was.

My two friends in Florida and my one friend in New York were walking this path with me from a distance, but the distance was difficult. I met another minister from my prior denomination at this time; and, while we were friends, I could not tell her the full extent of my sense of hopelessness and despair. I suspect she knew, but could not, as a new friend, know my history or the depths of despair to which I descended when in such a place. I spent my days and nights, many of them shaking from fear and anxiety, with my little Finian and learned again of the power of healing from this tiny little creature.

While I continued to attend services at both communities, despair and hopelessness plagued me in my now solitary life on an isolated mountain road. My interaction with Finian was often all that kept me going through those long days and nights. Finian and I began to travel locally. There had always been animal 'angels' in my life at the toughest times and my Finian made sure to stick close by.

Two aspects of my historical experiences in my spiritual journey reminded me it was possible for me to stay present in this life and to continue to search for the peace and tranquility I so deeply craved. From the time I was a small child literally being watched over and cared for by my childhood protector dog through other cats and dogs that wound their way in and out of my life, my love for and connection to animals sustained me through my roughest times. I began with increasing fervor to explore the spirituality of all of nature and every animal. I returned to my childhood beliefs as we traveled these roads and I began to remember that all animals, plants, and other natural phenomena have souls and that there is an over-arching power organizing and animating the material universe. This began to lay the groundwork for my future interest in and work in Shamanism.

Despite the beginnings of the crisis that would later lead to the complete collapse of my mind, body, and spirit, Great Spirit was continuing to work in me and prepare me for things to come. Nevertheless, I was exhausted, anxious, depressed, and not at all sure I could go on until my friends arrived from Florida. I thought often of suicide mostly because I just could not imagine beginning again. It all seemed too much, and I was too weary to wind my way through that tangled path. I was beginning down a long spiral of depression and fear. I would not reach the bottom for several months. My spirit longed for something more, but I was out of options. In the end, my dog, who would have been completely alone, and the refusal to hurt my family and friends kept me from acting on my thoughts. But those thoughts encased my heart most of the time. Surprisingly so and wonderfully so, my spiritual consciousness of the whole of the Universe did not fail me, and the energy of those around me—near and far, even though they did not know it—maintained my energy in my stead so that I could survive. Of course, I had to change my definition of 'survive' but it worked. Spiritually, I was hanging on by a thread.

At first my plan was to continue to develop my support system in Asheville and make every attempt to rebuild a life there. I did not believe that I had the financial ability to leave. As I worked to make this plan a reality, anxiety and depression came close to overwhelming me. The only thing that saved me from myself at this time was the readily available amazing natural beauty of the Blue Ridge Mountains and my dog, Finian, who now traveled the Blue Ridge Parkway with me as often as possible when I would go driving to save my sanity. I managed to stay connected with people by taking Fin to a dog park at the same time several days a week and running into the same dog 'parents' on those days. I never even knew their names (though I knew their dog's names); but they became a lifeline to other people beyond my part-time job. When the anxiety and depression became so bad that my hands shook all the time, I couldn't sleep, and I quit eating, I woke up one morning knowing I had to return to Florida. Once I made this decision, relief set in even though I was completely overwhelmed by all I would need to do to come 'home' to Florida. I began the protracted process of selling as many of my belongings as I could and planning to drive a U-Haul truck back to Florida.

My friends from Florida had previously made plans to visit me and so they turned that visit into a rescue mission to help me pack and stay steady enough to get through it all. One of them helped me in my packing and the other one kept my dog to save him from the craziness of watching his home disintegrate into boxes and less and less furniture. Several weeks after their arrival we began the long drive home—they in their motor home and Fin and I in a U-Haul towing my car. In all honesty, I do not know how I made it, except that they were there at the end of each day, with food, company and a safe place for me and Fin.

Disintegration, Diagnosis and Beyond:
Inside the Web

After my truckload of stuff was in storage, I stayed with these same friends as I sought an apartment or some sort of living situation. Relatively quickly, I moved into a senior living complex in a nice apartment. I experienced panic about living there; but I saw no other options. I set up the apartment and hated every moment I lived there. Although I spent a great deal of time looking for work, I filled my days by walking my dog around and around the apartment complex. Many, if not most, of the occupants were considerably older and in need of care. The anxiety over whether I could remain in that place began to grow. Spiritually, I was bereft. I again questioned Whomever was listening, 'What is wrong with me? How did I get to this place in my life?' No answers came, and I felt deserted from every spiritual experience or peace I had ever called my own.

Exceptional levels of anxiety seemed to arise with no warning. I grew restless and horribly depressed. I could not sleep. I tried homeopathic pills to get some relief from the anxiety. I awoke every morning and paced for hours trying to convince myself that I could handle my current situation. As I paced, I would pound on my chest so hard that I would sometimes leave bruises. I was becoming even more obsessive about certain things such as turning off the stove or whether I had locked the door when I left. Sometimes it would require two trips back to my apartment to give me enough assurance to leave. I felt as though I had no access to Spirit at all even though I had returned to Mindfulness Meditation to calm myself. It rarely worked.

My same dear friends became increasingly concerned about me. I was at their house often, but it was obvious I was eating almost nothing and that I was slowly coming unhinged. Although the chronology is a bit of a blur for me, I eventually returned to their home for what I thought would be a day or two. I saw a doctor who initially prescribed medication for anxiety and I tried to return to my apartment. Mornings continued to be unbearable even with the anti-anxiety medication and I began to have a harder and harder time getting through the day. I was afraid I could not take care of myself or my dog, so I eventually told them I could not live alone. I returned to their home for a much longer time than any of us thought. I saw the doctor repeatedly. She added some medications and I began the long journey of seeking a medical solution. She once asked me if anyone had ever told me I might have Bipolar Disorder, but I initially rejected the idea.

My days at my friends' home consisted of sleeping extraordinarily little, crying until sometimes 11:00 in the morning and eating only enough to keep me out of the hospital. How they managed to live through all of this remains the greatest mystery of my life; but it was the most significant gift anyone has ever given me. I finally saw a nurse practitioner at a psychiatrist's office, and she began to experiment with medications as well. By now, I had determined that the diagnosis of Bipolar 2 was likely and was spending hours (mostly late at night) reading up on all I could discover about the disorder. The experimentation with medication continued and life was a constant roller coaster. Some of the side effects were more than I could handle and some plainly dangerous.

Although it may not have looked like it, I was desperately trying to reconnect with some spiritual meaning in all of this. I tried meditation but could not control my racing thoughts. I tried to read, but initially was too anxious. I feared that I was doomed to stay this way forever. I saw no hope for peace or understanding. My worst times continued to be early morning and the hours just before sleep overtook me when my anxiety about having to wake up the next day kept me awake far into the night. Interestingly, even before my meds were stabilized, I was truly a different person from noon until about nine at night. I could relax a little, but my exhaustion was mind-numbing.

Throughout all this uncertainty, my dear friends kept watch, sometimes monitoring the constantly changing and confusing medication protocols, and encouraging me to eat. For months they provided all the care for my dog and for me and gave me the safety that I so desperately needed. I do not believe I would have been able to stave off suicide, and certainly not hospitalization, had they not cared for me in the loving way they did. I doubt I realized it at the time, but I came to understand that I was undergoing a deep spiritual experience through their profound love for me. First, I was, for the first time in my life experiencing unconditional love from these two amazing women. Secondly, I was, rather than ending the pain, allowing myself to endure it in the embrace of the safety that their love provided. I was learning to trust. Some may argue I had no choice; but I know that I did. And in and through their love, which was intensely spiritual, I made the better choice. I do not know of any other experience that would have opened my heart up to what would come after this time of initial healing began than my time in their home. To say that the anxiety in the morning was incapacitating would be an understatement. Even after I was somewhat stable on my medication, I would need to get up and take anti-anxiety medication at 5:00 a.m. and try to go back to sleep so that I was less shaky and able to start the day. I knew I had turned a corner when I stopped asking them if they would care for my dog should something happen to me.

On Christmas Day, I found out I was going to be a grandmother and for the first time in months I experienced tears of joy instead of pain. Soon after, I became quite anxious about what my illness would mean as I became a grandmother, my lack of finances, and my relationship with my son. However, I truly felt the joy and waited in anticipation for the arrival of my grandson six months later.

I finally happened onto a medication regimen that worked as well as it could. While the anxiety was more under control, and daily morning hysterical crying stopped, I was still quite fragile. This process had taken months. In the beginning of my emergence from my days of exhaustion, anxiety, and despair, I slowly began to take over my dog's early morning walks. Those block long walks were about all I could manage to do in the mornings at first. I finally began to go out for short trips and even returned to driving my car when my anxiety was under control. Spirituality re-entered my life in the form of returning to mindfulness meditation and reading inspirational works mostly by Buddhist or Buddhist-like writers. Not too long after this, one of my two friends encouraged me to take up billiards to get me out of the house and involved in something that might provide me pleasure. I quickly developed a love for the game (much more quickly than I developed the skills I needed) and it became a source of healing and meditation for me. It would continue to be integral to both my recovery and my hope to return to a 'normal' life.

I began to make plans to leave their home and found a house-sharing situation with a lovely woman who sometimes rented out a room at an affordable rate. Living in someone else's home was not what I had envisioned for my retirement; but I appreciated the ability to stay in my home community and for her welcoming spirit (and the fact that she liked my dog). Several months passed before this opportunity was available and so my friends continued to support and love me. I grew less suicidal as the medication became more stable and as my body began to heal and strengthen. Around this time, I also returned to the devotional writing I had been doing on my website and posting to Facebook after an almost 8-month hiatus. This ability to write again gave me great hope. Although it was extremely difficult to leave their home, I knew I had to try to live on my own. I told almost no one the nature of my illness and worked very diligently to appear 'normal'.

A few months after I moved into my new living situation, my grandson was born. I had not planned to see him immediately; but my two wonderful friends again came to my rescue and we planned a RV trip close to where my son, his wife and now my grandson lived at the time. I spent almost 10 days loving him and trying to get to know him as best I could. Many of my concerns about my relationship with my own son surfaced and I had some difficulty with anxiety while I was there. Mostly, however, my medications kept me stable and I was able to enjoy their family. I was completely at ease with my grandson and felt none of the decades old concerns about my (grand)parenting qualities. Leaving him was hard, but I was able to distinguish between natural sadness versus depression. This was progress.

There are times when I continue to be quite disheartened about my situation. I have begun to admit that I am angry and despairing about the circumstances that my unpredictable illness has left me in my so-called 'golden years'. From my quite limited perspective, I sometimes wonder why all the other people I know seem to be enjoying their retirement and I am living mostly in a single room, with no spare money, trying to stay upbeat about my life. My depression has not gone back into hiding and there are times when anxiety continues to dominate my thinking. I continue to experience PTSD from my childhood with the added PTSD resulting from the Bipolar episode that changed my life at 63. Panic attacks continue but I have learned new methods of dealing with them (including a medication specifically for that purpose) and now understand that they will run their course and end. The good news is that finally admitting I did not understand or casually accept my life as it had turned out to be was like loosening a steam valve. I did most of my processing alone because I had been unable to find a knowledgeable therapist; but at least I was processing.

Fortunately, during this early recovery, I was able to start attending groups about spirituality and to begin to get engaged in spiritual, recreational, and creative pursuits. I was gradually coming to terms with the impact of all that had happened. At first, I slowly and privately began to take a fresh look at the various traditions that had meant so much to me throughout my life and then began to focus on new traditions or beliefs that were surfacing in my hours of study as I was seeking for different ways to understand all that I had experienced in my mind, heart, and soul.

What I have learned most of all is that many things can be happening at the same time. My depression may linger, my anxiety may be mild or almost debilitating. At the same time, I am able to continue my study in healing practices and allow myself to use my skills as a healer with others. This is the crux of the nature of the web of spirals—they are interwoven and supported and challenged by each other. This is what leads us to experience many aspects of life and spirituality at the same time.

It was only after I began to find my feet again, that I felt as though I could breathe. I feel as though I have raced through my story and I am finally able to reflect on the changes in my life after diagnosis and appropriate treatment. I have noted before that 63 years is a long time to go without any diagnosis. Most people die from illnesses that are undiagnosed for that long, and indeed many of those who share my illness do. I have no explanation for why I made it this far except that, perhaps, my work on this earth was simply not finished. I am not brash or arrogant enough to suggest that I made it this far on sheer willpower. That is not only impossible, it is untrue.

When I first surfaced from what seemed a foggy, unknowable state of crisis, hopelessness, and despair, I thought I would immediately start to look for answers. Instead I found that, more than anything, my body and my heart needed to rest. And so, I did. I began to look for things to do, to get involved in, to re-enter the world, but for the most part, I rested. I did not feel guilty to be resting, I was grateful to be alive to do it. I learned to drive to the ocean, so I could sit by the sea and think. I learned patience in those days, knowing somehow it was key to my healing. This is not to say I did not struggle with the 'turning over'; or, at least, the 'not taking it back'.

As the days wore on, I learned that the ground was stable below me and that I could begin to wander down the path of discovery during my re-entry. I had come to believe much earlier in life that growth is always in a forward movement and that stepping backwards is some-how a negative thing. I found this not to be so. I found that after this spiritual awakening it was necessary for me to be quiet and wait for what would come next. It was important for me to be able to experience and deepen my growth and not just encounter 'aha' moments without life-lived context. I had to be willing to be flexible, gently moving forward; yet, having no fear for the backward steps when necessary. In this gentle dance of forwards, backwards, and sideways, I finally learned to move in Spirit and settle in stillness. The spirals became at least a little more predictable.

It became obvious that despite all my previous whirling dances of disintegration and reintegration, I'd never really had to make the kind of 're-entry' I found myself having to make. As I pondered before, perhaps it was because I was older, retired, and financially insecure. I was in the midst of 'normal' post-retirement adjustment—what to do next, how to stay active, where to find meaning in my life, etc. Of course, this was more difficult because I had retired sooner (much sooner) than I expected. The crisis that brought my career to a not so graceful crash landing as well as the beginnings (though I did not know this at the time) of my impending mental, physical, and spiritual collapse caused my retirement to come out of the blue. My retirement hit me like a meteorite that I did not see until it was too late to duck. I was completely unprepared in every way and I was knocked off my feet. I crawled on my knees almost another year trying to find answers to questions I had never contemplated and searched for ways to get back up. In the chaotic months prior to my collapse—two moves, one break-up, and the complete rejection by the denomination to which I had given my heart destroyed my balance and I could not find my way back to an upright position.

So, as I 'came to' from the almost six months of despair, diagnosis, and the beginnings of treatment, I was now dealing with the healing that my mind, body, and spirit demanded, as well as the 'post-retirement' questions that I had never answered. Initially, all I could do was get through the day. This came as a blow to my ego, my fragile self-esteem, and my heart. Most people with Bipolar disease are active people except for when they are not. I had experienced enough of the 'not' to last me the rest of my life. I wanted to be normal, to do everything everybody else seemingly could do. I wanted to put it behind me. With medication, I thought, I can be like everyone else. Truth forced me to take another, closer look at my situation after my life-changing disintegration and to admit that, even with the most artful integration, my heart, my psyche, and my spirit would never quite be the same. I also came to realize that, with time, that was an exceptionally good thing. I did not want to be the same. I wanted to embrace a new way of being; but admittingly, this was mostly abstract thinking at this point in my return to life.

I've found that while a few may understand, most do not. There are those times when 'getting through the day' is the best I can do and when I am in those times; I deserve to be proud of myself for doing just that. But I vowed not to remain there longer than I needed to. Even in my roughest times now I found myself yearning to be constantly open to living the full breadth of life even when the breadth held all the hurt and loss my heart had endured. By this time, I was beginning to make spiritual connections as my 'new' life unfolded. Knowing there was much to learn I became more open to deeper connection with Source (or Spirit) even when it seemed the silence was deafening. I was, in a slow dance with my soul beginning to know that while my life had been hard, my will to survive had been stronger.

I was slowly beginning to hope that there was a reason for all I had endured, not only in my most recent despair but in all the despair

I had encountered in my life. Somehow, I knew it would be a slow, ever-evolving process that would last throughout the remainder of my time on this earth. I wanted to have a purpose for the darkness that held me captive for at least half, if not more, of the time over the course of my life. I did not know what it would mean, but I knew that it was up to me to allow Spirit to work through and in me to reclaim my sanity, my life, and my passion. Parker Palmer, my spiritual mentor for years speaks of it in this way, 'If we are to live our lives fully and well, we must learn to embrace the opposites, to live in a creative tension between our limits and our potentials. We must honor our limitations in ways that do not distort our nature, and we must trust and use our gifts in ways that fulfill the potentials God gave us.'[4]

I knew my journey was about woundedness and healing. I reclaimed my place as a healer. I began to read of other traditions. Although I had done Reiki training decades ago, I completed Reiki training again including Reiki for animals. I was grateful to all the animals that had walked this journey with me. They inspired me. I studied about energy healing, reviewed all I knew about chakras and began to study the Native American and Celtic worldviews and Shamanism. I began to know that while my path would never be straight or narrow, I was headed in the right direction. I continued to study and to grow even while I was recovering from the most painful period of my life.

I don't think I have ever heard anyone say, 'I think I'll go explore the darkness today!' And, yet, day after day, I find myself doing just that. When I began to make that exploration and to know that at the other end of my vulnerabilities lay immense potential for love and wholeness, then facing those vulnerabilities became the most important thing I could do in the moment. Throughout this time of beginning to face where I had been, I was led inward and propelled outward to risk and risk again. And, in the risking, I found Love.

Even as the symptoms of my disease continued to make life difficult and I would find myself spiraling back into despair (which is deeper and darker for me than depression), I could also begin to explore those symptoms as vulnerabilities and mine them for strength and courage. The outcomes of bad decisions and unexpected life circumstances made the tentative steps back up the alternating twisting and turning pathways difficult and challenging. But I persisted, sometimes just so that I did not let down the women who had given so much to me; and sometimes because I could not let myself down having come this far. I was not ready to quit this time (though in my darkest moments I still wrestled with the question of the 'worth' of this pain and struggle); so, I pushed myself (sometimes into hysteria that I managed to hide from everyone but me) and refused to give up. The whirling thoughts seemed unstoppable, and sometimes, unmanageable; but I somehow made it to the point where I could begin to look at specific spirals of pain and disintegration which made it less difficult to find the connections and coherence for which I was looking.

7

The Not So Gentle Truths about My Experience of Mental Illness

As I began to re-enter life in a truly meaningful way, I began to explore that which I shared with many others—to find community—whether theoretical, virtual, or social. It required me to be willing to look at the most unbearably hurtful aspects of living with mental illness.

I believed that I was a fraud as far back as I can remember. Even though I managed (right up to the end) to maintain employment, have activities and community, I lived my entire life 'waiting to be found out'. My belief that I was not who or what others thought that I was, was constant and unrelenting. It is integral to who I am and who I perceive myself to be. It was always easier to tell people that I was 'shy' rather than admit that my social anxiety made it practically impossible to interact with people in a social environment. Because I lived in communities where social isolation was not a possibility, I had to find a way to interact with that community. For me, it was true that attempting to 'belong' when I did not feel that I belonged at all caused me to adopt a persona which was out of alignment with my deepest self. Once this lack of alignment became a part of all that I am, it began to destroy any hope for a sense of wholeness. And, like most everyone, I craved that sense of wholeness to feel complete.

I've spent a lot of time 'putting on a front'. All I wanted to do was to fit in and I knew that the only way I could do that was to aim for 'normal'. I always jokingly referred to myself as an overachiever, that is I believed that I had achieved more than I ought to have been able to because of my limitations. I now know that this was part of my 'fronting'; but it allowed me to stay employed, to keep friends, and, sometimes to have significant relationships. Hiding who I was and what I needed allowed me to save my tears (most of the time) for when I was alone—driving in the car or lying in bed trying to sleep. I felt rewarded for hiding who I really was. At the time when I needed others the most, I surrendered to my fear of rejection and walked bravely on at great cost to my mental and emotional psyche and spiritual heart.

Feeling that I was a 'fraud' or 'inauthentic' cut to the heart of my desire to be open and available to my friends, co-workers, family members, or new people with whom I wanted to form any kind of relationship. I did not trust who I was so how could I possibly trust others. Spiritually, I was unable to feel loved by the Divine, the Holy, or accepted as a valuable and vital part of the Universe of Love.

Every aspect of my life was affected by this notion that I was a fraud. As one brief example: As an adolescent, I began to sing in public as a soloist. This seemed something I was able to do with some aplomb. However, my belief that I was a fraud permeated this one source of pleasure. I began my obsession that, one day, someone would be brave enough to tell me that I could not really sing on key and that I should stop embarrassing myself and my family. It may seem strange that this would be the obsession of a young woman who financed her college education with a vocal scholarship, but the readiness for that revelation stayed with me for decades and troubles me at times to this day.

My various careers, including my time as a scholar, were filled with the same sense of 'pretending' and I waited in every endeavor to be 'found out' as the inept and incompetent person I believed I was. I had no way of knowing that this was a significant aspect of mental illness, particularly mood disorders, anxiety, and depression; and, so as I waited to be 'found out' as a sham I suffered greatly. The exact nature of my work life is not particularly important except to acknowledge that, in hindsight, I was quite successful. It is unlikely that I could have been so had I really been the kind of person that I believed myself to be, but by the time I began to have any faith in my true abilities, the damage was already done. Sadly enough, I simply did not believe that I had anything to offer the world, even when the world sought to show me otherwise. The sense of being a fraud was one of the most life-crushing and joy-killing aspects of my journey within the spirals of mental illness.

The spiritual aspects of this permeating feeling of being 'found out' are, in many ways obvious. Since I could not bring myself to believe that I was worthy of love, concern, or compassion from 'mere mortals' how could I possibly believe that the totality of the Universe would welcome me into the fold. This profound sense of separation from not only the rest of people but also from 'All Their Is' was spirit and soul numbing. Once I began to understand that it was my disease that taunted me with the split between fraud and Spirit, pretending and Center, I began my spiritual journey home.

For me, the feeling of failing to be who I thought I should be arose directly from the stigma and then shame attached to having a mental illness. Many books have been written about the role of stigma in the lives of those like me who contend with the disease of mental illness. Because stigma exists against someone like me publicly, it is not a far leap for me to take that stigma inside, make it my own, and then find myself engulfed in the horrible shame that accompanies my unconscious internalizing of everything that I hear about 'people like me'. I don't talk about my disease and find that most people I know will talk about almost anything, intimate, even inappropriate things, before they will use the words 'mental illness' in a meaningful way. It's unusual for me to be in a social setting where anyone shares of their involvement with mental illness or the experience of one of their friends or family members. I feel as if speaking about mental illness in 'polite company' (that's what my mother used to call it) is simply not acceptable. I figured out quickly that I should tell only a few people. The upside of this decision is that it caused me to become more cautious concerning those with whom I share the intimate details of my life. In other words, it helped reign in the mania which affected my ability to make good decisions about friends and relationships. It would not be unreasonable to suggest that the publishing of this book makes my past refusal to divulge the nature of my illness irrelevant. In sometimes quaking shoes, I have come to terms with the significance of the publication of this work.

I am angered by the hundreds of thousands of 'arm-chair psychologists' who, while uninformed, render diagnoses for those who do not behave according to society's norms. I am not suggesting that some people who commit violent acts or other dangerous acts are not suffering from one of many forms of mental illness. However, the reverse is not true. The clear majority of those who are mentally ill never commit any violent acts or engage in dangerous activity (except perhaps activity that is dangerous to themselves). Nevertheless, little acknowledgement of this reality occurs in reporting these attention-grabbing events. In fact, I believe that it is safe to say, that the occasions a reporter takes the time to differentiate between the perpetrator of the current act of violence and the rest of us who have a mental illness is statistically non-existent. That is just how strong and powerful the public prejudice is against people who have profound mental illnesses. So, I and all of us who deal with mental illness daily are subjected to additional stigma when distinctions are not considered. I believe that every time a violent act is attributed to mental illness, another brick is placed upon the wall that keeps me separated from those who consider themselves immune to mental illness.

This all leads or at least can lead, to shame—a profoundly emotional and spiritual phenomenon. While some might say that shame is a part of mental illness, I do not. I believe that shame is a natural, though not beneficial, response to all that I have described above. I grew up in a familial culture that reinforced societal stigma. I was a bright and precocious child in many ways and learned how important it was for me to 'fit in' at all costs.

I'll be the first to admit it. I'm not always charming, I'm not always pleasant, and spending time with me may be a burden for a friend or family member. I have come to understand that and no longer (at least most of the time) find myself resenting what I used to describe as lack of interest, care, concern, love—you get my point I can be difficult to get along with and I may be in a place where I get frustrated easily or angry for what appears to be no reason. However, most, if not all, people with a serious illness do the same. It seems, though, at least to me, that it is somehow easier for people to find their compassionate selves when an illness is obvious or physically debilitating.

Carrie Fisher, until her death in 2016, was one of the first celebrities to go public in a bold way regarding her Bipolar illness. She said, "One of the things that baffles me (and there are quite a few) is how there can be so much lingering stigma with regards to mental illness, specifically Bipolar Disorder. In my opinion, living with manic depression takes a tremendous amount of balls. Not unlike a tour of Afghanistan (though the bombs and bullets, in this case, come from the inside). At times, being Bipolar can be an all-consuming challenge, requiring a lot of stamina and even more courage, so if you're living with this illness and functioning at all, it's something to be proud of, not ashamed of. They should issue medals along with the steady stream of medication."[5]

Feeling like a fraud, internalized stigma and shame all played a role in my feeling that I needed to pretend to be something that I was not. My mother, because of the culture in which she grew up and the social norms of the South which she adopted when she moved there from the Mid-West, raised me to determine my actions by two principles: Is it the right (just, moral, ethical) thing to do and what will people think' if you do it, or speak it, or be it'—whatever the 'it' was. The first principle was easy. Regarding the second, I learned and re-learned throughout my life that I did many things that caused people to think things that my mother did not want them to think about me, about her, or about our family. While it was frustrating and hurtful beyond belief, I do not blame her for living into her own history. Nevertheless, the concern about 'what people would think' worked poorly for me and I would suggest is at least one of the bases for my internalized stigma and shame. Unfortunately, my experience of stigma and shame caused me to hide, particularly during my darkest hours, my most terrifying hours. I did not want people to hear or see me in those moments because I feared their reaction and I feared my own feelings about being 'found out'. This dangerous combination has left me in some extremely perilous and dangerous places in my life. I am grateful that this life-threatening illness did not become life-ending for me although it nearly did on several occasions.

Stigma is a profoundly spiritual issue. I wanted to believe that Oneness includes all that I am, not just those parts that 'fit' into some preconceived pattern of acceptable behavior. However, believing that this 'Oneness' does not include me because of some diagnosis or set of behaviors does almost irreparable damage to my soul. If I do not recognize and name internalized stigma—that belief that I somehow 'deserve' the derision, discrimination, and alienation—it can, in its powerful thought process lead to the killing of my soul and, perhaps my life. Prior to my understanding of internalized stigma and the role that it has played in my life, it forced me, unfairly, to contend with a multitude of spoken, written, and sometimes physically aggressive violations of who I am as a human being. Society plays a sinister role in internalized stigma. It, society that is, expects me to act as if living with mental illness is not burdensome or leaves me unscathed. In the minds of those who do not understand the severe impact their behavior has on my journey I may even be expected to give them some assurance that their behavior is somehow acceptable and respectable—neither of which is true.

This phenomenon of public shaming and derision leaves me with the task of rejecting that shame, of refusing to take it into my core and to accept that I am who I am and that, in some ways, I must live without society's understanding, compassion, or grace. This leads to a splitting off from who I know myself to be—a kind and generous person who longs to fulfill my life purpose and passion just like everyone else. Spiritually, I develop an even greater sense of shame that separates me from my yearning to recognize the Divine within me.

Then there are the issues surrounding suicide or attempted suicide. Even admitting to experiencing suicidal thoughts rarely generates compassion or understanding. I remember with great love and gratitude, a dear friend who was mostly paralyzed, in constant pain from MS and a spinal cord injury and had no medical hope for a functional life. She was ready to die; in fact, she had a 'stash' of pills sufficient to end her life available at all times. I knew this and encouraged her to talk about it and deal with it in the open at least with me if she could not with anyone else. Her grown children also knew of her stash although, clearly, it was harder on them to know of it. When she learned that her last hope at pain relief was medically impossible, she felt that she could not go on. In the end, she did not use her pills as she contracted a deadly infection, suffered from sepsis, and refused medical treatment. She transferred to Hospice and they cared for her as she made her transition from this plane to the next. Not a single time did I hear anyone suggest that she should have fought harder, kept trying, or refused to give up. At her celebration of life, person after person praised her for having 'fought the good fight' and 'given more that any human being could be expected to give'.

I use her story (She was both a friend and a retired psychologist, and I know she would approve.) to illustrate the difference between physical reasons for ending one's life compared to mental or spiritual reasons. When one attends a service for a someone who has been successful in their suicide attempt, there is little understanding that they 'fought the good fight' as well. Often the cause of their death is a 'hidden' thread throughout the service out of respect for the family who cannot deal with the reality of suicide. When someone tries suicide and fails, they are in a precarious position regarding the reaction of those who love them or know them. Relatives and friends may whisper the reason for their hospitalization and empathy and sympathy are in short supply.

I believe that the topic of suicide may be one of the last taboo subjects on the planet. This is stigma; and, therefore, when taken in, is internalized stigma at its worse. It could cause me along with others to deny my deepest desperation for fear of rejection and contempt. What is so tragic is that this lack of support at my most desperate hour would be the very thing that I needed the most. Can any of us imagine standing vigil at the bedside of a person with severe depression and anxiety who has chosen to stop their suffering by refusing treatment and end their life at their own hands. Unlike in the case of my friend above, most of us cannot endure the thought of it. This utter lack of ability even to imagine such an act is the most extreme consequence of treating mental illnesses differently from physical illnesses.

For me, medical intervention and psycho-therapeutic treatment is linked to internalized stigma and shame. However, those topics also carry my greatest ambivalence and gratitude simultaneously. It was, of course, medical intervention, which both saved my life; and, for a while at least, greatly increased the hell through which I was living. This is true throughout my lifetime when misguided diagnoses caused me to take medication which I did not need and had significant negative effects. It was true for me even as a child when the doctors who I saw either did not see or refused to see that abuse was damaging my fragile mind. It was true in my adolescence when I first became addicted to early anti-depressants and 'nerve pills' (for my anxiety) and pain medications for the aches and pains caused by depression; and, it was true as I began this last uphill climb back from hell. Of course, the ambivalence arises from the fact that these interventions saved my life and made it possible for me to fight another day.

From my perspective, psycho-therapeutic interventions suffer from the same ambiguity and inconsistency. I felt dismay when three of the therapists I saw after my diagnosis, informed me, they really knew extraordinarily little about Bipolar. Most referred me to books which I had, of course, already read. In a thoroughly sarcastic moment, I brought one therapist a 3-page bibliography of books on Bipolar, many of which I had already scoured for self-understanding. Another psychologist informed me that because I had procured my own psycho-education there really wasn't much for her to do. This was all during the time when I was desperately trying to put my life back together and plan for my future now that I understood my diagnosis. I tried to contain my fury at their inability to see my desperation, but sometimes it slipped out anyway.

I had several psycho-therapeutic interventions earlier in my life as well. When I finally ended up in the hospital at 17 weighing 68 pounds I was, of course, released into the care of a psychiatrist. His 'cocktail' of medications made me too ill to eat, so I won that battle and opted for chocolate milkshakes instead as a way of maintaining my weight at 80 pounds. As I recall, he wanted to talk about my sister and mother, and I wanted none of it. I just wanted to feel whole again. At some point, I cycled out of this horrendous depression without further intervention and resumed my late adolescent life. I did not understand, obviously, the cyclical nature of my disease. At this point my Bipolar had not evolved into Rapid Cycling and so there really were times of relative stability in my life—some call those periods of calm remission, for me it was more like transient relief from symptoms. Several more therapists made it into my life, a marriage counselor or two, and, much later, a significant psychologist in New York. I worked with her for almost 8 years. Although she watched me cycle in and out of depression and anxiety many times over those years, my diagnosis was always clinical depression and adjustment disorder. Of course, although I was on and off medication—all anti-depressants—none of them were appropriate for Bipolar issues. Nevertheless, she walked me through processing the worst of my abuse issues, my PTSD, and supported my attempts to make sense of it all.

Even though I remain committed to finding a therapist who understands mood disorders and is willing to face my pain with me, so far, that has not happened. Not long ago I terminated my fourth therapeutic involvement in the 3 years since my diagnosis. Below are portions of a statement I read to her as I was ending treatment. The original statement was much longer, but these are the significant parts. The words are important not just of describing this most recent 'therapeutic' relationship but as a synthesis of all my attempts at therapy since my diagnosis. I am not proud of my anger; but my despair was real and terribly, terribly important.

'I've come today to tell you why I don't think there is any good reason for us to continue. Here's what is true for me. I have found that therapists, for the most part, don't really want to hear about the hell of Bipolar. You seem to fall into that same category. In fact, it doesn't seem to me that you want to hear any of my story at all. You are content to see me as functioning and stable enough to merit no real concern. You don't want to hear about how I sob and scream into my pillow at night, trying to figure out how my life turned into this living hell after working so hard my entire life. ... You are happy to hear that I am getting out and doing things again. That is enough for you because you don't really want to hear how hard my life is, how desperate I am at times, and how difficult it is, despite appearances,

to make it through the day. ... How about telling me that you admire me for not taking my own life when that would be the far easier thing for me to do. You could be honest and tell me that you have nothing that can ever really help me in my daily struggle to make the most out of my life. You could tell me that you respect all that I have done with my life (although you know little of that) despite the cycles of depression, anxiety, and mania that I have lived with since I was 17. ... It's plainly important for me before I walk out this door for the last time that I make one last attempt to get you to understand what all this means, if not for me, perhaps for the next time someone comes to you in this kind of pain.

I was a counselor for years, saw all kinds of people and kids and addicts. I learned several things that you apparently did not learn. I learned that to tell someone with compassion that you are sorry for all that they are having to go through means the world—doesn't change anything of course but can make all the difference in the depths of despair. I learned that if I was to be of any good at all to those sharing their pain with me, I had to be willing to hear it, accept it, acknowledge that there was no explanation for why they must suffer and agree that, yes, it was indeed unfair. I had to be willing to take their pain into my heart and make some effort to make sure that they knew I genuinely cared about their daily and hourly struggle. I learned that being willing to let someone thrash around in their pain and trust that they were safe with me was the most healing thing I could do. Be their safety net even for that one hour. ....

You don't know what it is to feel the walls closing in at a time when all that you worked for is denied. Perhaps in your opinion I should be satisfied that I am back doing some of the things I love; that I am giving to people, that despite it all, I am a healer and a writer and a friend to those who need me. And I am grateful that my spirit is alive and can be used in that way. And it gives me a way to truly help when someone is in pain. I'm grateful for that and know that all these things can be true at once. I just needed one place where I thought I could be the rest of who I am, the scared, confused, ashamed, and hopeless about my future person who longs for the kind of retirement for which she worked her whole life. I am certainly competent, but I am also broken-hearted. I certainly lived a successful life, but I have little left to show for it...

And so, I'm done, I'm spent, and I'm too tired to try to make you understand any more of this. ...living my truth means that I must speak my truth. And I have.'

It does not take much analysis to hear the deep spiritual nature of my explosive rant. I was desperate and this particular therapist not only had no assistance to give, her lack of compassion and caring was palatable. The powerful outcome from all these attempts is my renewed commitment to helping many find alternative ways to understand their own lives, their journeys, and the healing ways awaiting them. Because I embrace the gift of being a wounded healer, I bring a distinct perspective to those who yearn for healing and hope, and out of that commitment arises a personal power all the uninformed therapists in the world could not have shown to me. This spiraling into rage and despair allowed me to find a new purpose and bring me to the top with renewed energy and hope.

Little Whispers of Acceptance

When I first began my journey after my diagnosis, I, quite frankly, rejected the notion of acceptance. I simply did not and could not accept my illness, my circumstances, or my life at that point in my journey. And, as an aside, I think anyone who thinks that acceptance comes at once or close to diagnosis has not studied mental or physical illness very well. After a diagnosis which took over 60 years to discover, therapists, doctors and other well-meaning people began talking almost immediately to me about acceptance before I was stabilized on medications. Not only did I not know what it would mean to accept this illness, I could not process how acceptance was the key to whatever living with this disease would look like. I responded by simply refusing to believe that I needed to accept it, since I didn't know what that meant.

Giving up on the notion of acceptance for the time being, I began to look for other ways to explore the topic. I had no difficulty believing that I could, in fact, be walking along my journey when suddenly, seemingly out of nowhere, a violent storm would be upon me. I had lived through storm after storm after storm. I was initially unable to describe the storm—the terrible depression, uncontrollable rage, shaking anxiety, and what seemed like a series of unbearable losses in my life. In some ways I had developed plans for dealing with the storms, but they varied in success. My years of searching for an authentic spirituality had indeed left me unprepared for such a storm perhaps because I had learned to live from one storm to another. I began to understand that my current crisis (the illness itself) was not separate from the spiritual crisis that I thought I was avoiding by insisting that I was not angry or resentful—Because I WAS VERY ANGRY.

It occurred to me that one of the things that contributed to my difficulty was my long-held insistence upon perfection. Despite, or perhaps because of, my feeling that I was not an authentic, valuable person, I was a closet perfectionist. I would give others second chances, but certainly not myself. I had a tough time accepting that I could neither control nor make perfect my circumstances. Though I resisted, I began to realize that I could not be perfect and fully human at the same time. My perceived imperfections were thrown in my face, and duck as quickly as I could, I could not avoid the mud. I slowly began to at least contemplate that I was at a particularly important turning point. If I could embrace all that I now knew myself to be, my strengths and my limitations, I could allow a sacred transformation to take place and come to know the whole and complete person that I was called to be. Acceptance, when it does come, usually comes, or at least it did for me, in tiny little whispers of 'it will be okay', 'I can do this', 'I will be shown the way', or, later, 'I believe in myself and love myself enough to give it a go'.

This does not mean I did and do not slip back into despair at times. Acceptance is a back and forth movement between affirmation and denial, acknowledgement, and refusal to see. Acceptance is not a one-time event. Though the moving away from acceptance comes less often now; it still comes. I find myself, when I am having a day that is full of anxiety or sadness, or when I am having trouble doing the things I want to do, saying 'this is the nature of the disease'. And, deep inside, if I listen closely, I may hear the voice of my inner distress saying, 'but, does it have to be this way?' It is then that I must welcome my distress, hold it, love it, and make sure that it—that I—know it is okay to want to say 'no'. Because giving myself permission to say 'no' leads me back to the place where I can open my heart to embrace all that I am. And, here is the spiral again, pulling me downward only to fill me with the strength and grace to courageously surface with a newness of belief in myself and my ability to live my life as a full and successful person.

I can admit without self-judgment that my initial acceptance was simply 'acting as if'. I was well into my study of new spiritual practices and reviving some that had been meaningful prior to my intense period of depression and anxiety before I began to live into a spiritual—and not just behavioral—understanding of acceptance. However, as I acted 'as if' I accepted and understood the symptoms of my illness, I began to realize that I could weather the crises that still arose. I stopped look- ing for ways to overcome it, stopped wishing for a 'do-over' and just kept moving. So, acceptance is not saying 'I give in', it is saying 'this is what is'. Some great mystical experience of ACCEPTANCE is neither realistic nor useful. I learned acceptance and continue to do so day after day, both emotionally and spiritually and that learning has been a great gift.

I take great comfort in Elizabeth Kubler-Ross' statement: "The most beautiful people we have known are those who have known defeat, known suffering, known struggle, known loss, and have found their way out of those depths."[6] And so, I came to 'yes'. And, yet, I knew that to continue in my understanding I would have to delve further into my vulnerabilities and strengths. Looking at my vulnerabilities requires courage beyond the everyday kind. It takes the willingness to go into the forest without a path, or to swim in deep waters without a lifeline. There are times, quite frankly, when I have been unable to release my perceived security even for a moment. I refuse to be too harsh on myself in those times. Learning to develop that kind of courage is growth itself. It is a circling path, of course. The more I relinquish the perceived notion of control, the more I open to growth. I am meant to grow, even in those times when staying snug under the covers of mediocrity would 'feel' so much safer. I continue to struggle but I have developed a sincerely profound commitment to growth and relinquishing security for a time to ensure that it has simply become a part of the process.

I have come to understand that when I find myself amid chaos or confusion and I am in a time of great spiritual pain, I can surrender to the depths of that pain or I can refuse to acknowledge its presence. I doubt at those times, maybe even a lot, about whether the Universe knows what she is up to. I want to know why I can't always seem to find immediate access to feelings of unconditional Love. I experience loss or, perhaps, re-experience it when ramifications of a years ago unwise decision hits me where it hurts, and I still question. It has, however, come to me that I can question and still embrace the 'yes' I have chosen to say to Spirit. When I embrace all that seems to overwhelm my spirit, I am created anew. My experience in this time of confusion serves me well when the next one arrives. I discover new levels of compassion and kindness to those who find themselves in similar spiritual circumstances. I learn to allow my immersion into new depths of spiritual self-awareness, and I celebrate the courage to love myself into rebirth and renewal. For one thing, I have allowed myself to ask, mostly alone in my car at the top of my voice, 'why me?' Rachel Naomi Reman, gave me a model for the beginning of my path to acceptance. "An unanswered question is a fine traveling companion. It sharpens your eyes for the road."[7] And so I began down the road with an unanswered question, a question with many parts and many answers and I knew I was on my way.

First, I had to start with understanding the impact of my disease on my life. And, I strongly believe the longer your mental illness goes undiagnosed and untreated the more difficulty you will have with acceptance. There is, quite frankly, so much more to accept. I found that regrets about the past kept me from moving into a positive place. Kay Redfield Jamison, in her ground-breaking book and movie, confirmed that with which I was beginning to struggle. She says, "It took me far too long to realize that lost years and relationships cannot be recovered. That damage done to oneself and others cannot always be put right again".[8] I, myself, had been spending hours each day agonizing over things I simply could not change—money I had wasted, relationships lost, my inability to raise my son, scholarly pursuits lost in a haze, self-harm, abuse endured, dreams denied or abandoned—the list seemed endless.

My first step toward acceptance then became the releasing of the notion I could somehow 'make things right'. Raging against all I had done to myself and to others only delayed the time when I would begin to walk forward. Slowly, and I mean slowly, I began to let go of the regrets, shame and 'what ifs'. This does not mean it is not a painful, excruciatingly so, process. It is. Regret is painful. There are simply things we cannot retrieve. We cannot restore time. We cannot know what opportunities would have been ours. I discovered that this is hard for those who do not live with mental illness to accept this as real pain, saying instead, "this could be true for anyone". It could be, but there is a particular despair that I experienced as I came to terms with the fact that the majority of my losses were mostly due to the symptoms of a disease over which I truly had little control.

My first visit to see my new grandson brought all these issues to a head. I struggled with how little I felt I could bring to the role of 'grandmother'. His other grandparents were in a completely different situation and I felt inferior in every way. While I came to understand many things in that process, I struggled to find my worth as a grandparent. Of course, the first time, that little boy (and two years later, a little girl) smiled at me, many of those thoughts vanished or were no longer important, but they surface from time to time leaving challenges that are difficult for me to work out.

Amid dealing with the 'what ifs' and the 'whys' I began (only began) to recover a truth I had once glimpsed at another time in my life. The energy I spent wrestling with the various 'whys' for the situations in which I found myself, sapped my strength and sabotaged my courage for the explorations that truly mattered. Growth demands that we understand and embrace what is primary in our spiritual lives--deepening our relationship with Spirit to live out our purpose in the world. This insight propelled me to begin to deal with where I was in the here and now. In tiny little steps I began to move toward resolution with the ambiguity that laced its way through my pathways and yearnings for explanations. But those steps were minute, slow, and incredibly painful. And far from finished.

I have learned that my mind sends me a consistent signal when I am slipping away from acceptance. It is a quite useful reminder, although it can be quite painful. Every time I find myself with the thought 'this is a dream, that my life has come to this, and I will soon wake up' I realize I have fallen away from acceptance and taken a step toward denial. Of course, when I realize that I will not wake up and that it is not a dream at all, I must begin again with acceptance. Over and over I find myself on the path TO acceptance instead of the arrival AT acceptance. Spiraling through this process of learning to accept that at an age of close to 70 years, I realized that I simply do not have the time to restore all that I wish I could. Coming to terms with the toll the past 65+ years has taken on my life, in every way possible, is exhausting, leaving me panting with fatigue and sometimes wishing for it all to end.

The rage that I was experiencing at all I had 'lost' in the past and present was in line with the self-hatred that was an integral part of my disease. It was clear to me it (self-hatred) was the first thing that had to go if I was to reach acceptance of my disease, my past, and my current situation. It was important for me to realize that I grew up in a world that encourages self-doubt and, in some cases, self-hatred because it (society, teachers, partners) told me I was never 'enough'. I would not begin to suggest that others do not experience this as well but when mental illness and the mis-firing of my brain impacts the way I process things, I long ago took this inability to be 'enough' all the way into the deepest corners of my heart. It is integral to my disease.

It is a supreme act of self-compassion and spiritual revolution to agree with yourself to be 'enough' just the way you are. This does not mean one should continue in obviously unhealthy habits and patterns of behavior, but it does mean that until I can come full circle to loving myself enough to change for my highest good, what I am is 'enough'. When I come to the place of knowing all is well with me—even allowing for and encouraging change and growth, I will begin, slowly at first, to replace hatred with love as a first step to acceptance and peace. I had to learn to be gentle with myself because I cannot hear the acceptance of others if I cannot accept myself.

Living into my disease is intrinsic to my spiritual journey; I must listen hard to what my soul is trying to tell me. I must shut out the noise of others' ideas of who I should be, how I should act or what I should believe. I must also shut out the noise of who I thought I should and would be. In the end, authenticity and integrity is all I have. Whether living with disease or not, this authenticity and integrity is manifested in the Love into which I live. My soul takes me there and opens me to the painful and glorious reality of all I am.

I have faithful friends that gift my life with tender love, forgiveness, and grace. They are the ones who stand beside me because they believe in me no matter where I am in my journey. I have come to understand and embrace that as I allow people to see my soul, more of these loving people appear in my life. It seems so difficult to allow people to love the real me--the naked, imperfect me. I must, of course, start by loving my own soul. I have found the basic 'rule' of the journey is this: I cannot invite or even allow others to love me and journey with me until I invite my true, authentic, less than perfect self on my own journey. I had to journey alone into dark and scary places, spiraling down into darkness and unknown destinations before surfacing again into the peace found in lush green forests. Then I was ready for companions. Travel is so sweet with others; and, so gentle, too. It was necessary for me to know deep in my being that my call is to an unending commitment to myself. It only increases as my journey grows deeper and deeper.

My journey also requires me to accept that I need and require help from others. When I was at or close to my lowest points in my 'disintegration' a few years ago, I spent hours in the home of my friends, sobbing and rocking back and forth. Repeatedly, I would say, "I'm sorry, I'm sorry, I'm sorry". And, indeed, I was. I could not imagine that anyone could tolerate the total disruption of their lives by my daily hysteria and utter hopelessness. Throughout it all, they assured me I had nothing to be sorry for and they only wished they could 'do' something to relieve my pain. Many months later, when I was more in touch with feelings and thoughts, I wept for them; not only in gratitude; but, also in sorrow for the great grief they must have felt as they could do nothing but sit and watch me sob.

What a terribly exhausting path the friends and families of those with mental illness walk. With little to no support, they struggle to find the right words and actions, while at the same time dealing with their own lives, activities, work, and health. Caring for someone who is experiencing the storms of mental illness is an almost full-time job and no one receives a respite from their own life to care for another. The responsibility some perceive to 'keep another person alive' is not only unfair, it is impossibly unrealistic.

My dear friend in New York—I spoke of her before--bailed me out of several financial situations my poor decisions had generated. I never really knew why or how she loved me that much, but I accepted her help though I regretted deeply that I needed to do so. She has not stopped helping me in every way possible through this illness; and, although it is difficult for me to accept her love and care, I am grateful. There are others who have helped me, and I am sure there are more to come. Each time I must ask for help I am nearly overwhelmed that I am in such a position again. Allowing others to fully love and support me is not only an emotional issue for me, it is a spiritual one—filled with great longing and regret. It is an issue that returns many times for me. During my best days, I can also understand that it is a blessed opportunity to feel and accept the unconditional love that is generated by Universal Love itself.

9

First Steps: Return to Mindfulness, Meditation and Taoism

I spoke of my introduction to Eastern Religions while I was pursuing my Masters' Degree. I am grateful for this gift. It was useful to explore the role of Mindfulness, Meditation, and Taoism in my spirituality. I have practiced meditation for many years. In my yearning to understand what was going on in my fragile mind, I think I instinctively knew that mindfulness meditation could play a significant role. I used guided meditations in the 1980's and 90's at the suggestion of two of my therapists. I learned Mindfulness-Based Stress Reduction from a certified teacher in the mid-1990's soon after it began to be popular. Jon Kabat-Zinn remains one of the authors and practitioners that at least provided me with ways to approach the exceedingly difficult 'symptoms' of stress and anxiety in the years before I understood where that stress and anxiety originated. In the weeks when I was new to my diagnosis, I sought out and used guided meditations especially related to stress and anxiety. These were helpful both in the morning and at night. Mindfulness, itself, is a way of life, one which is both subtly derived from and completely coordinated with Eastern Traditions.

By practicing mindfulness over the years, I have become convinced I spent a great deal of time simply 'sleep-walking'—perhaps for a feigned protection from the magnitude of life. However, practicing mindfulness in meditation and throughout my daily life, the world and all that is in it simply took on new meaning. Once I began to integrate mindfulness into all that I did I learned to focus on the here and now. Mindfulness led me to the outer edges of the path on which I was walking. It called me to look closely at almost hidden movements I would ordinarily miss simply because I was too busy looking in another direction.

Mindfulness called to me to identify what was profoundly important and to learn ways to enter into deeper conversations with those aspects of my life that led me to declare my commitment to those things which matter most. In practicing mindfulness, I learned to allow feelings to free-float through my mind without granting them permission to take up residence in my life. This is an extremely difficult practice for me since my thoughts tend to percolate repeatedly in my remarkably busy head. Particularly in mania, mindfulness is difficult to exercise but it is a constantly evolving practice; and, it does, indeed, require patience. But it was gentle practice—moment by moment— that enabled me to fully embrace and allow what was already happening to simply happen.

Because I had spent time several decades earlier in significant study of mindfulness it was the first practice I turned to when my mind and heart were torn apart as I was propelled down into the depths. And it helped with the symptoms, some, but only some. Mindfulness does not promise that my situation would change. In fact, it does not promise that anything will change. To practice this form of meditation I must accept, without judgment, my present just as it is—that what is IS. I found that denying my present reality caused me to lose touch with my own heart and inner voice, while embracing the present as much as I could enabled me to stay more grounded. This was not foolproof for me, but it was a way to the reassurance of the breath, the source of life, the one constant in, what was for me, a very inconsistent world. Pain, then, is just pain; fear, just fear. Returning to the breath, I returned to the one thing that attached me to the center of my being—that life force within me.

For me, the most important aspect of mindfulness did not come in increased understanding of mental illness as a spiritual journey; but rather, the impact of the concept of mindfulness in everyday life as a way to control some of the distraction and inability to focus that accompanies depression, fear and, especially, anxiety. Mindfulness then, was a significant part of my spiritual journey because it began to instill a sense of trust in myself, something I had never experienced.

Although Buddhism has informed my journey since I studied it as a graduate student in the early 1980's, Taoism is the Eastern tradition that most impacts my understanding of spirituality and mental illness. I have, since those earlier years, regarded myself as an 'unofficial' and, quite honestly, rather little-informed Taoist. But the barest of understanding made sense to me and I have been drawn to Taoism for the past 40 years. This current undertaking, in some small measure, has allowed me to not only study Taoism in some greater detail, it has also allowed me to apply those beliefs to my situation as I seek to make connections between such traditions and Mental Illness. In the days immediately after my diagnosis I returned to the study of Taoism, knowing that the emphasis on flow and non-doing might prove beneficial particularly in my search for a way to deal with my initial rejection of a diagnosis that shook me to the core of my being. In many ways, meditation and Taoism were the first places I found spiritual sustenance in the early days after my diagnosis.

There are some basic Taoist beliefs and those beliefs contributed to my understanding the flow of events in my life. Tao (the 'Way') is another word for Universal Life Force. Taoism does not differentiate between 'good' and 'bad'. Both are accepted and incorporated into the path of life. Life is to be lived simply and respect for all of life is crucial. Finally, life is a cycle much like a spiral. Taoism called me to always return to the Tao, the basic Source of Life itself. Simply put, the Way is both part of everything and greater than everything.

It's a simple set of beliefs. For someone like me who is living with mental illness, it can take on special meaning if I can learn to see my mental illness as a part of All There Is and, except for keeping myself and others safe, allow my feelings and circumstances to play out in accordance with the Tao. Lao Tzu says, the way of the Tao is to yield to life. In my journey I have begun to see the bending, shifting, swaying, yielding to the Universe in a beautiful interdependent dance among all that inhabit the earth and beyond. I cannot (and this shows my opportunity for continuous growth) seem to walk away from certain questions. For example, why when the great wind of change blows me off-center even if just for a moment before righting me again, do I feel such an urge to resist with all my might? Yielding to the Way of the Tao is the way of peace and contentment. Allowing my body to feel in the moment what I am feeling anyway, free from resistance and push-back loosens the hold on my need to control what is and frees me to experience liberation beyond my wildest imagining. And, yet, I struggle. Perhaps, for today, it is enough for me to simply recognize the struggle, to pay attention to all those thoughts that rise inside me--to lovingly and gently hold those feelings of resistance, of lack of control and chaos and to say, "I see you and hear you." Perhaps, this gentle approach is the key to my letting go.

And, again, I must accept the process of change. I grew up and now live again in the state of Florida. I have seen many hurricanes and tropical storms come and go. Many places in the world are hosts to hurricanes, typhoons, and tornadoes. I have visited the coast and seen groves of trees close to the ocean that the wind has blown to the ground so many times, they are permanently bent. But they are still standing. Yet in every storm, big or small, the trees that are uprooted are the trees that cannot bend with the wind. In the spirals of my changing life I can learn to be like the trees that survive, letting my heart, mind and spirit bend and sway, because they do not fight the storm that comes, they move within it. The next time I find myself amid some rough weather--and I will—I hope that I bow and curve, twist if necessary, and always, yes, always remain flexible within the storm. And when the storm has passed--and it will—I am still standing, stronger than before.

Based on my knowledge of Taoism, I find this is in fact, the most important thing the Tao leads me to understand about living with mental illness. I learn to bend and sway with it; to be able to say, "Damn, I'm having a rough morning today", but at the same time know if I do not fight it, if I just go with it, it will more than likely move on and I can carry on. When I surrender, I become one with the spiraling dance of wind and rain and will soon rise to the surface again.

10

The Roots of My Past: Christian Thought and Practice

From age seventeen forward, I yearned for—craved for, even—a way to 'fit' my spirituality into the terrible ins and outs of my life. As early as 1997, I thought I might be able to address such topics. I have found notes relating to earlier attempts of beginning a book similar to this one; but it was always obvious that I did not have the insight I needed to continue those projects with spiritual or psychological understanding. So those attempts went no farther than an outline or the beginnings of an Introduction because I simply had no ability to 'put it all together' no matter how hard or how often I tried. I continued to seek and as I longed for this cohesiveness, the paths I have followed have been painstaking; and, in many cases, painful. As tentative as these speculations may be, they are the beginnings of bringing meaning to a lifetime of mental and emotional suffering and spiritual confusion. My relationship with the Sacred is restored through this seeking; and, I am grateful beyond measure. I would agree with Joseph

Campbell when he says, "People say that what we're all seeking is a meaning for life. I don't think that's what we're really seeking. I think that what we're seeking is an experience of being alive, so that our life experiences on the purely physical plane will have resonances with our own innermost being and reality, so that we actually feel the rapture of being alive."[9] I spent the first 60+ years of my life so alienated from that rapture that I could not even see it in the distance.

As a younger theologian I was often confused because various traditions use different vocabularies to describe both the way the world and cosmos is viewed as well as distinctive meanings of 'healing'. I struggled, as I authored this book, for ways to keep those various vocabularies from becoming too confusing, but I am sure there are places where I have failed. Growing up in a mostly white, mostly evangelical, or conservative, wing of Christianity, I did not have any exposure as a young person to any belief system other than 'Christian norms'. The paranormal was off limits, mediumship, psychic abilities, or any belief system that even touched on magic (which included any kind of energy healing) were considered evil and should be shunned. Eastern Religions represented cultures which Christian churches regarded as 'mission fields' where people needed to be 'brought to' Jesus for salvation. African tribal culture was especially disrespected as missionaries flocked to Africa to 'bring the Word' to 'heathen' countries.

As I said in a much earlier section, I want to say again that what was true for me in the negative impact of Evangelical and Moderate Christianity in the understanding of mental illness is only my truth. And while I maintain several significant beliefs regarding Christianity, my debt to Christianity in my spiritual development has been undeniably significant. Nevertheless, I find it particularly wrong to ignore the colonialism of Christian missions which was and is an insult to the rich and meaningful history of traditions of non-Christian cultures and the great gift they bring to the world. Secondly, the increasing need of some 'Christians' to believe that they have the divine wisdom to determine what is Christian and what is not has become hurtful beyond measure and has threatened society in general and, my spiritual life, in countless ways.

I now have great compassion for myself—this budding theologian who tried for almost a lifetime to find a way to incorporate my experience with Christian traditions. I now understand that I wanted, almost more than anything, for those 'Christian' beliefs to be the core of my belief system as I made new and different forays into other ways of understanding the world and, specifically, my place in it. I wanted my new, and initially frightening thoughts to both begin and end in the depths of a belief system to which I had devoted most of my life.

Nevertheless, my journey has taken me through many twists and turns both over the years and since the episode that finally led to proper diagnosis and treatment. Because of my early involvement in Christianity and my significant education in that tradition, I always believed that there was a spiritual component to my depression and anxiety; but I had no way to express that other than to look at my 'failure' to embrace the healing that Christianity 'should' have brought to all my troubles. But I was struggling to do just that. Sadly, in the midst of living through and with the symptoms of my undiagnosed Bipolar Disorder, Generalized Anxiety Disorder, Panic Disorder and PTSD I searched for meaning, any kind of meaning—spiritual or otherwise. For the most part, I simply could not see purpose or hope at all.

As I re-examined much of what I had studied and learned about Christianity I wanted to explore certain aspects of Christian theology that were and are particularly important to my understanding of healing. While mostly a hold-over from earlier days (seminary and graduate school studies), I studied the writings of 20th and 21st Century Christian writers who fit the definition of a 'mystic'. These writers bring a profound expression regarding life's struggles to the discussion of Christianity and mental illness. I also looked at the Christian tradition's two most prominent ancient mystics, St. Theresa of Avilla and St. John of the Cross. As I have come to study other traditions, I have also come to a better understanding of ways in which Christianity has influenced me in profoundly positive ways, beyond the negative experiences I endured as a child, adolescent, and young adult.

I believe that the experience of being a mystic is universal. I never even contemplated ignoring what I believed to be a 'call' to ministry. This was my first expression of my earlier call to become a healer. Within the confines of my spiritual rearing thus far, it was the only choice that made any sense at all. Upon allowing some of what I had learned in seminary and elsewhere to surface as I searched for ways to connect with my Christian upbringing and education, I remembered my study of the Dark Night of the Soul. I also remembered my significant discomfort in my study of this Dark Night. Even at the beginning of my study, some 40 years ago, such an experience made sense to me, but there was something terrifying about it that I cannot now quite remember. Perhaps, it simply reinforced my own struggle to incorporate all that I knew on an academic level with all that I knew on a psychological level.

Now that I knew the identity of my battle, perhaps I could re-examine what I had previously learned. Instinctively, I knew that an understanding of this Dark Night was crucial to understanding the interweaving of spiritual crisis and mental or emotional crisis. I turned to Gerald May, remembering from seminary that he is one of the leading authors concerning the Christian understanding of the Dark Night of the Soul. Christian scholars and mystics have most often marked the emergence of the discussion of such a phenomenon as beginning with the writings of St. John of the Cross (1542-1591) and St. Theresa of Avilla (1515-1582).

I was somewhat relieved to find that May suggests that St. John of the Cross has been wrongly interpreted. He states, "the dark night of the soul, in John's original sense, is in no way sinister or negative. It is, instead, a deeply encouraging vision of the joys and pains we all experience in life." [I used to believe that the 'dark night of the soul' was a one-time event after which I would have some deep understanding or communion with God. Since I experienced this 'one-time' event many times, I was convinced that I had not yet reached the depths of what would be considered a 'Dark Night of the Soul' that would produce the deep insight, understanding, and coherence for which I longed. Though I experienced crisis after crisis, it appeared to me as though I could not even discover the proper level of spiritual disintegration that I needed to set my life aright.] May suggested, however, that this 'night' can occur at various times throughout our lives. And there is no guarantee, that once it has occurred, a person will experience a lifetime of ecstasy and joy. In fact, he warns us that it may return at the most inconvenient of times. Theresa echoes these feelings. She says, "I am convinced that instead of being a once-and-for-all experience, the dark night of the soul appears in numerous ways throughout our lives, always mysterious and always hopeful." May summarizes the thought of both writers: "For Teresa and John, the dark night—indeed all of life—is nothing other than the story of a love affair: a romance between God and the human soul that liberates us to love one another." [10]

When I take seriously that the 'dark night' is a continuing, spiraling engagement with the Divine, I find that I have a new way to describe and experience those times when God seems to have deserted me. The dark night is a mystery then—one which I certainly did not understand at the time I was engaged in my earlier study. As those dark nights deepened, even in my confusion, I longed to know that there was a process going on and if I could just grasp the nature of that process, I might get a better grip on what was happening to me in those times when I could see nothing but a great wall of darkness between me and God. When I could not hear God answer, I would then know that I was experiencing one of those 'dark nights'. It seemed as good an explanation as any to my fragile and confused mind.

So, I interpreted my dark nights as the descent into despair and depression. I, as one of the graced ones, have always come out on the other side, but I realize now that I was always changed. I understood myself, others, or my place in the world differently than prior to my 'dark' experience. As I re-interpret (as many mystics do) these periods as significant parts of my spiritual journey and not just the overtaking of my tender spirit by a force beyond my control, I begin to see the significance of these periods in my life. Even during these occurrences, I began to look for hidden clues (and they may be hidden beyond conscious recognition) to the meaning of where I was in my life in that moment, and those dark nights became less threatening and life-extinguishing.

Realizing my own humanity, I began to wrestle with the nature and purpose of my struggle. This is the brokenness that I somehow knew I must embrace if I were to welcome the call of 'wounded healer'. For me, one of the most solitary aspects of dealing with mental illness is the feeling of complete aloneness in that dark, though mystical, place. I have loved the words of Parker Palmer, Quaker mystic, since I was in seminary and he has been my spiritual hero since then when I first read *Let Your Life Speak*. He has long spoken openly and honestly about his depression and the profound impact it has had on his life. He describes his depression as a way that his psyche (although he does not use those exact words) is trying to get his attention. I do not believe that Palmer is just talking about depression, I think that he is talking about a process that enables me to encounter the spiritual and take part in spiritual growth even as I struggle with mental illness. I have come to understand that life-long mental illness such as that which I contend will always be present in one form or another. This is nothing more than fact—just as my diabetes, glaucoma and arthritis will always be present. This is not a statement of defeat. It is just so. And, with all these physical illnesses there is much that improves not only my quality of life but also my availability to participate in all this as spiritual journey. I do not remember that this brought me much comfort the first time I engaged with the words of Parker Palmer, but I can see now how integral this kind of understanding is to the exploration of meaning in the web of life.

Much later in his life Palmer wrote *A Hidden Wholeness; The Journey Toward an Undivided Life*. Palmer says: "I pay a steep price when I live a divided life—feeling fraudulent, anxious about being found out, and depressed by the fact that I am denying my own selfhood. The people around me pay a price as well, for now they walk on ground made unstable by my dividedness. How can I affirm another's identity when I deny my own? How can I trust another's integrity when I defy my own? A fault line runs down the middle of my life, and whenever it cracks open—divorcing my words and actions from the truth I hold within—things around me get shaky and start to fall apart.... Wholeness does not mean perfection; it means embracing brokenness as an integral part of life."[11]

I find great meaning in the notion of living such a divided life because that is exactly the way I have and would describe most of the first six decades of my life. And the toll it took on my heart, my spirit and my body is beyond words. I tried many avenues to escape this 'split' between who I appeared to be in the world and who I knew myself to be. I believe it is quite common for those with mental illness to attempt to live this kind of divided life—to try, hard as they might, to appear 'normal' in a world which, if it knew the truth, would not consider them normal at all. Coming to this understanding enabled me to put into context the almost life-long belief that I was not who I said I was. I found the ability to love, and embrace, all the years of struggle and to affirm the strength of character and grace it required to survive such an existence. This is an immensely spiritual experience. What a relief from guilt and shame I would have known if someone had explained to me that I was simply trying to make my way in a world that made it almost impossible for me to survive.

And, so, I come at least partly full circle; and, certainly deeper into the spiral of understanding when I re-interpret depression and despair in these ways. It took courage to bring fresh eyes to that which has been a part of almost every day of my life in one way or another. The opening of my heart and mind to ways of seeing myself, others, the world, and all that is in and part of it, is the story of the rest of this book. I am grateful that I am here to write it and mature enough to know that the very same thoughts I just expressed in the paragraphs above are part of the reason that I am present.

PART TWO

11

The Nature of the Healing Vortex

Energy is a spiral in constant motion. In fact, without Energy, Life Source of the Universe, we would simply cease to be. With each day of healing from my own crisis I was able to explore various aspects of energy and healing work; and while I had been interested in energy work—particularly the harmony of the chakra system and the healing methods of Reiki—for decades, I was finally able to bring some cohesion to my thought. In my journey, the use of many forms of energy healing formed a foundation for understanding my condition when I was finally able to do so. I am indeed a practitioner in some of those same modalities.

As I practiced various methods of energy healing, my heart began to surface from self-doubt and disillusionment, and I began to remember my lifelong truth that I am indeed a healer—though a wounded one—and began to integrate that reality into my greater understanding of life's spiritual journey and mental illness. Attempting to focus on the myriad of energy healing methods all at once is not helpful or possible so I began by returning to my knowledge of Chakras and Chakra work.

This was not the first time I had looked at this system of spinning, whirling discs of energy deep within and without my body, but it was the first time I felt that my well-being demanded a greater understanding. My first knowledge of Chakras, though substantial, came from my 'Yoga period' in my 40's and 50's. I built upon that earlier experience by exploring in much greater detail the role of chakras in overall physical and spiritual wellbeing and balance.

I continue to discover that there are as many names for the process of removing blockages from the energy flow in the body as there are understandings of how that energy flow works. In the years that followed my significant study I learned that the name is not what is important. What became important for me was to develop the ability to travel through my body in thoughts and feeling and find where the energy or ki (chi, qi) has slowed the spinning of the energy centers or caused them to come to a screeching halt. When I reopen those places, gently and lovingly removing the walls that I, for many reasons, have developed, I can literally feel the energy begin to flow again. I have experienced this surge of holy energy both as a physical process resulting in a pulsing surprising flow through various parts of my body that have felt sluggish, or as an emotional or spiritual process where I feel myself come into alignment and I find myself moving in one direction with single purpose and process.

There are many Energy Healing modalities and all focus on the health and healing of the energy that swirls within and around our bodies, minds, and spirits. Most importantly, I have experienced firsthand that Energy Healing does not focus on only one condition. Regardless of the modality, Energy Healing is a holistic way to understand and address the many energetic blockages that may delay healing or simply make it difficult for healing to occur. I know that there have been times when my body wanted to heal and yet something was 'cutting off' my innate ability to heal myself. For me, the experience of early trauma was particularly impactful on my ability to heal. Emotional or mental stress, or a myriad of other issues (that may appear unrelated to the specific issue at hand) often mean that I must look at more than one area for both self-healing and in my healing work.

I found that one of the most useful principles of Energy Healing as I dealt with aspects of mental illness is the concept of 'grounding'. Grounding strengthens a connection to Mother Earth and the energy contained in the earth itself. It "establishes a smooth flow within a central energy column running from head to feet and interpenetrating with the physical body, increases your sense of gravity, and gives you balance."[12] Not only does the practice of grounding enable the healer to tap into the flow of universal energy, it can also give the person who is receiving the treatment a sense of being centered and solid. As I deal with mental illness, the ability to 'ground' and 'center' is a skill that can save me from becoming lost in the chaos that sometimes appears during an episode. If I can allow myself to draw energy from deep inside the earth, I will be able to return to a state of stability and calm. While this may not immediately appear to be a spiritual practice, the ability to connect with Mother Earth and draw strength and centeredness directly from her is soul-restoring in the true sense of heartfelt spirituality.

Although I had studied the Chakra system decades earlier, I found the need to revisit and review what I already knew. These seven wheels of energy 'circulation' must remain balanced. Cyndi Dale, notes that "The chakra system is a seven-leveled philosophical model of the universe…A chakra is a center of activity that receives, assimilates, and expresses life force energy."[13] In the traditional understanding of chakras, these spinning wheels of energy begin at the root of the spine and proceed upward through the body to the crown of the head. Chakras are like the locks on canals—each one must open for the energy to flow through. If one chakra is unbalanced, blocked, or unable to spin so that the energy can flow through to the next chakra, the body cannot heal. This dysfunction makes it impossible for energy to flow in life-giving fulness from one chakra to the other, blocking the pathway of the Universal Life Force. These blockages do not exist in isolation. When one chakra is not spinning in clear lightness and energy, it is likely that one or more other chakras are also out of balance causing the body to feel off-center, lethargic, and unhealthy.

In her description of each chakra, Ruth White tends to focus on the emotional aspects which are especially important in understanding the role of chakras in the seeking of greater integration of body energy when exploring mental illness. I have shortened and adapted her material while trying to stay true to her words. The connections made to mental illness in the discussion of each chakra are my own and should not be attributed to Ruth White. My comments are in italics.

The root chakra is found at the base of the spine. Its primary role is in providing our body with 'rootedness'. White writes, "This is in some ways synonymous with 'grounding'. In accepting incarnation, we become rooted in the element of earth and more consciously interactive with the life of the planet. The more we are rooted the less does life on earth become a burden. Difficulties take on a new perspective, giving us more over-all purpose and sense of meaning."[14] Each chakra contributes a color to the vibrational energy field of the body. The color of the Root Chakra is red.

I have found that it is the Root Chakra that holds my power of self-preservation. Therefore, instincts which relate to my survival on all levels reside in my root chakra. According to experts, the health and balance of the Root Chakra is very much determined by the experiences I may have encountered in my early years. The meeting of primary needs (those needs which are necessary for survival on this planet) must be met for the Root Chakra to develop well. Although, I had little understanding of the world around me at this early stage, my emotions were accumulating memories and mine were certainly not pretty. It is easy to understand why the lack of the fulfilling of some of these primary needs may have contributed to my sense of 'not being a part of this world'.

The second chakra, which contributes orange to the energy field of the body builds on the rootedness of the first chakra. The sacral chakra is concerned with security and sense of others. *The more 'rooted' I am in the first chakra; the more security and safety will be reflected in the second chakra. My perception of my own insecurity more than likely turned into fear or uncertainty. This creates an imbalance or blockage in the second chakra. I don't know that I ever felt secure in this world. Doing Second Chakra work enables me to view others as less threatening. It helps me feel safe and secure and frees my emotions to explore my creativity and growing sense of self.*

The third chakra, yellow in color, is most often called the solar plexus. The solar plexus is the center of the ego and relates to digestion, vision, and psychic energies. If I say that I feel as if I have been 'punched in the gut' I am probably talking about feelings generated by the solar plexus. *It is in the solar plexus that children develop the ability to say "I" and know what they mean by that. From here comes my sense of identity. I have always known that this part of my body was involved with the feelings around my experiences in the world. I felt 'empty' and longed to fill my belly with love and a sense of fulness of life.*

The heart chakra is the fourth chakra. Compassion and understanding reside here. One learns wisdom and transforms the basic emotions of the heart chakra into healthy feelings in our lives. It is in the heart chakra that one is able to experience feelings without having them control one's life or sense of responsibility. There it is possible to learn the meaning of the word 'tender' and begin to become tender with ourselves and with others. The color of the heart chakra is green. *I think the Heart Chakra brought particular challenges for me in my mental illness. I felt disconnected from my heart, afraid of feeling and unable to find ways to express feelings in positive ways and to find forgiveness for myself. I longed for empowerment that is born in the heart chakra. For me, empowerment (no matter how many classes I took or books I read) seemed extremely far away indeed.*

The throat chakra belongs both to the lower chakras which help me find my place in this world and the upper chakras which relate to my spiritual development. This is where the ability of expression lives. This is where children first 'find their voice' and where they come to connect to that which is special about themselves and be able to convey that to others. The throat chakra also serves as a gateway to the upper chakras and the spiritual qualities that exist in the fifth, sixth, and seventh chakras. The energy color of the throat chakra is light blue. *I don't know about others, but I felt very out of touch with my throat chakra. I had little way to be true to myself or to express who I knew myself to be. I could not identify realistic expectations and my ability to speak up for myself was almost non-existent. I had difficulty knowing the difference between truth and untruth given that my own reality had been challenged so many times by different abusers and those who mistreated or doubted me along the way. My communication skills were limited except in academic areas and I had few ideas about how to express what I wanted or needed.*

The brow chakra is located between the eyes and is sometimes referred to as the 'third eye' chakra. It is related to Spirit. "According to its nature, 'spirit' is difficult to define. It is often confused or contrasted with 'soul'. One of the aims of the [ancient art of alchemy (the transformation of matter—spiritual or physical)] is to cause a mystical marriage between spirit and soul. Spirit is thus seen as clear, direct, and initiating, while soul is receptive and gestating...The spirit seeks completeness, commands action to enable it, and fertilizes inspiration and insight. ...Within each one of us there is a spark or essence which never gets clouded."[15] This energy center produces the color indigo to the spectrum of color in the human energy field and is the chakra that propels the human to instinctively seek for harmony between body, mind, emotion, spirit and soul. *As a person with mental illness, my feelings and hurts may be stuck in one of the lower chakras which leads me to great frustration because my energy seems to be unable to reach the sixth chakra. It is here that I learn that it is necessary for all the other five chakras to be in balance and swirling as healthy vortexes of energy before I can fully understand or embrace the brow chakra.*

Finally, the crown chakra is seen as "a clear chalice in which the spark of the spirit can burn as a strong flame. This image represents the consummation of the mystical marriage and the birth of knowledge, light, vision, healing, and wisdom."[16] It is in the crown chakra that a trust in true knowledge is found. This trust in higher insight or the higher self brings with it a trusting attitude toward life and the belief that all in life is working for our greater good. *This is a challenge for me; a challenge I believe is born of the lack of security I have experienced in the world, a lack of trust that I was living in my authentic being, and a lack of a basic knowing of self along the way. The sense of being a fraud which*

I spoke of earlier makes it virtually impossible to trust that what is coming through the higher self is Truth and Beauty.

White describes the healthy being as "a radiant, rainbow being. Part of healing intervention is to detect where this rainbow radiance may be faltering and to channel healing energy so that a subtle luminosity is restored. When our subtle energies are radiantly full of light and rainbow color, this penetrates through the body, mind, spirit, and emotions, and manifests in vitality for life." She continues, "Healthy chakras and auric colors look like stained glass when sunlight passes through it: fairly intense, bright, and translucent."[17]

Ambika Wauters, in his valuable book on Chakras as archetypes reminds us that this is a journey of progression. He tells us that "we cannot leap from the Victim to the Guru and expect to remain at that elevated level if we have bypassed other aspects of ourselves. Until we have worked our way through all archetypal stages of development, life will bring up situations that will force us to pay attention to any parts of ourselves which need healing and transformation."[18] Further, he warns against being judgmental or employing self-criticism. His words make perfect sense yet are profoundly difficult for me in my daily living with mental illness. However, these words can serve as a worthy goal: "By being loving and gentle with yourself you can avoid falling into either judgment or criticism. Self-acceptance and love are the keys to growth. [You are] learning to develop and integrate [your] life experiences in a way that will strengthen [your] spirit[s] and sustain [you] through difficulties and challenges. This is one means of working out old and negative patterns of behavior that have limited you in the past."[19] Being loving and gentle with myself is rarely easy, if not almost impossible, but it is a vital part of the sacred transformation I am experiencing.

There is, of course, much more to the reality of energy healing than a simplistic study of chakras although it was a good place for me to start. As I progressed in my study of energy healing, I began to understand energy as a spinning vortex of movement and therefore change. At first, this vortex felt frightening, given my experiences with tornadic explosions of uncontrollable feelings and reactive behaviors and the sheer will that it takes to remain alive in the midst of these vortices. I slowly began to understand this swirling energy as the source of all energy, and, therefore, as the source of the energy that would heal me. Over time, I began to see that all healing happened inside the healing energy vortex and my fear was overcome by experience.

12

Reiki Energy Healing

Within the many methods of Energy Healing, Reiki began to take on more importance in my thought and, eventually, practice. While my first study of Reiki was decades earlier, I was unable, in the weeks immediately after my collapse to bring those 'concepts' to bear on the issues surrounding my mental health diagnosis. Since completing my Reiki Certification and exploring multiple expressions of Energy Healing and other methods of healing that fall loosely under this category, it has been highly beneficial to begin to practice this method of energy healing on myself and others.

In a beautiful description of Reiki, Anne Samson says, "Reiki is a way of bringing us back home, of re-connecting with the essence of who we are. Reiki is a way to remove the veil that prevents us from experiencing the union with the divine. As we begin to wake up to this idea and walk its path the veil becomes thinner and thinner. We begin to see that it was our fears and beliefs in limitation that created the veil in the first place. So, Reiki is a doorway that can re-connect us to the very place we came from. Reiki is a doorway home".[20]

Like many healing modalities, self-healing is crucial to becoming able to bring healing to others. This is the way to becoming a channel for healing energy to flow. As tempting as it is to skip the work that it takes for me to make progress in self-healing, it is important to affirm its value, not only for my own health and well-being but for those for whom I serve as a conduit for healing energy. Reiki creates a place of harmony and balance.

Leading Reiki expert, William Rand describes Reiki: "Reiki can be defined as a nonphysical healing energy made up of life force energy that is guided by the Higher Intelligence, or spiritually guided life force energy. This is a functional definition as it closely parallels the experiences of those who practice Reiki in that Reiki energy seems to have an intelligence of its own, flowing where it is needed in the client and creating the healing conditions necessary for the individual's needs."[21]

Reiki is an energy healing technique that originated in Japan. It is a method that technically could be administered by 'laying on hands' but the practitioner's hands do not have to touch the person who is receiving the treatment. It is the passing on of Life Force Energy from the Source of Universal Energy through (and not 'by') the practitioner. The Japanese word 'Reiki' is formed of two Japanese words: Rei which means 'God or Divine' and Ki which is 'life force energy'. So, Reiki really means 'spiritually guided life force energy'. Reiki is simple and safe. It is considered a complementary healing method which means that ethical practitioners do not dispense medical advice, give diagnoses, or advocate that those who receive Reiki should stop any current medications or treatment.

Reiki is simple to learn, and classes allow students to gain and refine healing methods and techniques. The ability to practice Reiki is imparted when an 'attunement' is given by someone who has studied and become a Reiki Master. This allows the student unlimited access to an infinite supply of life force energy to pass on to their 'clients' or to themselves. While there are specific hand movements used by most practitioners, the passing on of energy is not dependent on those specific movements.

Reiki is not a religion. There is no dogma and nothing the practitioner or recipient of Reiki must believe to either give or receive Reiki. Even so, it is still important to live and act in a way that promotes harmony with others. Mikao Usui, the founder of the Reiki system of natural healing, recommended that one practice certain simple ethical ideals to promote peace and harmony, which are nearly universal across all cultures. During a meditation, several years after developing Reiki, Mikao Usui decided to add the Reiki Ideals to the practice of Reiki. Their purpose is to help people realize that healing the spirit by consciously deciding to improve oneself is a necessary part of the Reiki healing experience. "For the Reiki healing energies to have lasting results, the client must accept responsibility for her or his healing and take an active part in it. Therefore, the Usui system of Reiki is more than the use of the Reiki energy. It must also include an active commitment to improve oneself for it to be a complete system. The ideals are both guidelines for living a gracious life and virtues worthy of practice for their inherent value."[22]

There are several ways to phrase these principles. I prefer to keep it simple: 1) Just for today I will not worry. 2) Just for today, I will not be angry. 3) Just for today I will do my work honestly. 4) Just for today I will give thanks for my many blessings. 5) Just for today I will be kind to my neighbor and every living thing.

When I returned to my Reiki studies, became a Practitioner, and found a community and other places in which to practice, I felt as though I had found what became my first of four connecting tribes. I knew I belonged, and I found myself relaxing and trusting myself for the first time as a healer. While this does not disparage all the other ways I have been a healer, this was the first time I did not doubt myself. There are three symbols Reiki Practitioners use that have been passed down from Mikao Usui. They are a power symbol, a symbol for mental and emotional healing and a symbol for distance healing. These symbols were true to my own journey and I felt as if I understood something at its deepest level (although I believe that I have many, many things to learn). What is important here is that I experienced it as a part of myself. Involvement in Reiki is particularly useful for those who struggle with mental illness because it does not advocate turning away from conventional medicine or treatment, and there is no judgment implied. There is no measure of success or failure either for the giver or receiver and it is impossible for me to enter into negative judgment about my ability to receive unless I choose to do so. This judgment conflicts with the basic principles of Reiki.

Reiki Master Lisa Powers speaks of the usefulness of Reiki energy in the releasing of memories and beliefs that no longer benefit us and to gain increased wisdom and growth in self-understanding. She states, "We tend to store energy in the form of memories and beliefs and as they accumulate around the same theme, the strong dissonance begins.... When a body receives Reiki energy, it is like having a light to make the body aware of the energy that is not serving it. The practitioner does not decide what needs to be released or when, the wisdom of the body does. The practitioner holds the space for the body/mind to see the possibilities it can choose from regarding healing, so the body is no longer tied to a dysfunctional way of being. Once the body has chosen what it is ready to address, it can systematically release the stored energy at a cellular level connected with the imbalance. The cells then begin functioning as intended and the healing occurs on a physical as well as emotional, mental and psychological level."[23]

During this emotional healing, the body does not need to be consciously aware of the beliefs and/or memories that Reiki is addressing. All the client needs to do is to allow them to fall away and resist the temptation to invite the negative energies back into residence. As the body returns to a more natural and whole state, inner harmony is restored.

Finally, it is not possible to overstate the impact on me when I allow myself to be used as a conduit of giving a treatment to another person. Tanmaya Honervogt tells us lovingly, "If you give or receive a Reiki treatment you touch something deep within yourself. You could call it your 'innermost being'. Reiki is really an expression of love for yourself and for others and, in tune with the heart, it generates healing. Also, your intuition becomes sharper with Reiki. You gain access to the potential that is buried inside you. Every person is capable of self-healing and Reiki is a wonderful creative 'tool' with which to access this ability."[24] Reiki showed me not only my ability to be used authentically as a healer but also to become my own self-healer. From Anne Samson, Karuna Reiki Master, "Reiki is a powerful practice that increases our connection with the Divine and helps us develop our spiritual gifts, including intuition, healing and love. When we use these gifts in our daily lives, we become more connected to others and provide healing in a variety of ways, more ways than we may be aware of."[25]

As I recovered from my worst of many episodes of instability, it was wonderful to come to an understanding that it was no longer necessary for me to deny who I am. I learned that perfection is not the goal; it is healing through Universal Source. Since I was the passageway through which energy flowed and not the source of the energy itself, I could bring my gifts to others while still (and always) performing Reiki on myself and inviting that Universal Energy through my guides and teachers to bring me into higher and higher consciousness. It is important to note that in Reiki the goal is not 'curing' but 'healing'. There are many ways to heal and to become whole. For my own spiritual (and I do consider it spiritual) journey Reiki provided extensive insight into the nature of healing itself and my role as a healer.

13

Singing in the Forest: The Ancient Celts

My Irish heritage has led me to a life-long interest in Celtic lore and the mystical magic that is inherent in that lore. Drawn back to the world of Celtic magic I remembered the fairies that helped me navigate a lonely and frightening childhood; and, was sure other mythical creatures existed as well. My earlier fear concerning others calling me 'crazy' no longer had a hold on me and I have been able to move from interest to application. The concept of living in more than one world and the validation of my earlier experiences of 'thin places' (places where the Divine was easier to access) helped me to integrate in a profound way my experiences along my path.

While my interest in Celtic Spirituality and the desire to study it in detail grew out of my Irish heritage, I became fascinated with its mythology, belief in the reality of three worlds, and relationship with nature. Nevertheless, I am going to have to leave the details of mythology and lore to Celtic scholars (of which there are many) and focus on the concepts that were the most helpful for me in understanding mental illness through a Celtic perspective. First, it is important to note that the Celtic lands, particularly Ireland, Scotland, Wales, and other portions of Great Britain, parts of Europe and other places are lands that have been occupied at some point in their history and their ancient practices have been co-opted in many places by the Roman Christians who attempted to quash the ancient beliefs. However, Celtic ways are never truly silenced; they just go underground, fortunately passed on to future generations through poetry, song, and myth. Much can still be learned, therefore, about Celtic traditions.

Because it is important to get a full understanding of Celtic traditions, it is useful to include a brief description of ancient Druidry, which was so integral and formational in the Celts connection to the earth. Unfortunately, just as with much of Celtic earliest history, much was lost, destroyed, or distorted by conquering invaders. Nevertheless, there is much we do know. Druidry is, more than likely, the oldest spiritual tradition of the Celtic World or, perhaps, the entire world. There have been resurgences in Druidry, only to be snuffed out again, throughout Celtic history. Druids now practice in Celtic regions and all over the world. More than anything, Druids believe in the divine connection between the land and the people who live on it. Druids do not have an external deity, though some are quite devoted to gods and goddesses. This is not universal, however. What is universal is the work that Druids do in bringing awareness to the importance of the relationship of nature and humans to anyone who will listen and commit to change. If you remember my fascination with nature and its healing powers throughout my life story, you can understand why I have always been drawn to Druidry.

Joanne Van Der Hoeven, in her book, *The Awen Alone: Walking the Path of the Solitary Druid* speaks of "gaining inspiration and wisdom from studying the patterns that nature is constantly unfolding around us and using that as inspiration for a more holistic way of life. At its very core, Druidry holds a reverence for nature."[26] Druids accept that they are accountable for both their actions and their environment. So, it is not merely about refraining from actions that negatively affect the environment, it is also about actual, physical caring for the environment itself. One might wonder then if many of the environmental activists, acting on behalf of the world in so many ways are not, in fact, modern Druids. Van Der Hoeven makes it clear that it is not necessary to belong to an Order or an official group. When one follows the commitment to the earth and all its inhabitants, they take part in Druidry if they identify as such. Van Der Hoeven unequivocally states "Druidry is all about working in the world, being in the here and now. It is very much a pathway that is based upon what you do, not what you say or what title and credentials you claim. It is experiential and physical."[27] I do not consider myself a Druid although I do believe that I am descended from an extensive line of Druids. This expands my spiritual growth by reinforcing my focus on the earth and natural things outside myself. I am also invited by Druidic beliefs to feel a part of something much greater. This connection between my inner life and my outer life in the world helped me understand that one is not separate from the other and therefore I am not separate from the world, but rather an essential part of all that is around me. As a person who has dealt with feelings of being separated from All There Is, I take great comfort in knowing that, indeed, I am inseparable from it. The hole in my heart created by the mis-firings of my brain is at least partially filled by this knowledge.

This same belief is found in the many festivals, sacred days, and sacred myths in Ireland and the other Celtic countries. These are all important to the Celtic understanding of human life, wholeness, healing, and transformation. Frank MacEθwen, one of the leading authors on the spiritual traditions of the Celts says, "The Celtic spiritual traditions are rooted in peace. Prayers, rituals, daily acts, and orientations focus on fostering peace. The Celtic spiritual path aims to facilitate three conditions: an opening within the human heart, a sheltering sense of solace in the world for those who struggle, and an ongoing sensual celebration of the beauty of life."[28]

Elsewhere, MacEθwen shares his belief that one of the things that sets Celtic Spirituality apart is the mutual longing for sacred knowledge. "What you long to know seeks to be known. What you yearn to manifest has its own longing to be created and brought into form. What we long for wants just as much to be discovered, found, or expressed as we do to discover, find, and express it."[29] So I come to know that sacred knowledge which already lives in me can be trusted. Trust has never been a reality that has been available to me before and knowing or beginning to know that I can trust the sacred knowledge that lives within me is a step in a very right direction.

There is nothing more sacred and revered in the Celtic Tradition than the tree. I see that the holiness of my childhood in nature is connected to my attachment to trees. I loved them. I love them now, and through them ancient unseen doors open. Celts are lovers of trees. In fact, the religion of primal ancestors is centered in the mysticism of trees. Trees are magical with healing and other properties attached to each different type. Instinctively, I knew this, and my earliest art focused almost entirely on trees. Even my drawings of other things, cottages, castles, landscapes always appeared through the branches of trees or featured trees nearby. My fondest memories of my grandmother's house are of lying on the ground under the giant maple trees that surrounded her home as I gazed up through the ever-shifting branches. My 'hiding' place was under the great weeping willow tree that grew in the midst of what my grandmother (with more than a slight exaggeration) called the 'orchard'. My parents named my childhood 'home' (a four-room house made by my mother's and father's hands) 'The Sycamores'. One of the only positive memories I have of activities with my father was going mushroom gathering at the base of trees throughout an unknown mossy forest.

While I did not know that my fascination with trees may have grown from my Celtic heritage hidden deep in my cultural DNA; I do and always did search for the tree that served as the 'Tree of Life' in every forest I visited. It would always show itself to me, the largest and broadest tree, usually close to the center of the area through which I walked. I am certain that I never brought a 'Garden of Eden' understanding to these trees. Somehow though, I intuitively knew that the center of knowledge, the key to the knowledge for which I had always yearned was hidden in the reality of those trees. Mara Freeman, another Celtic scholar, writes this about the Celtic Tree of Life: "The Tree of Life can teach us about turning our visions into reality. When a tree grows, its first task is to establish a root system, to create a foundation that will support its upward growth…. Unless we are 'grounded' at the beginning, it will be impossible to soar ahead at a later stage. The tree develops because of the myriad complex, interchanges that take place among its roots, branches, and leaves and with nutrients in the soil and air. … As the tree brings up nutrients through the roots to nourish its visible portion, we draw the inspiration from the soul into our everyday lives. But the growth of the tree also depends on the sun, rain, and air. So, our dreams must also be exposed to the analytical scrutiny of the mind, which helps us figure out ways and means and solve problems; to discriminate between what can and can't be done, what is and is not working."[30] As someone who was continuously and passionately looking for sacred presence those trees were beacons of that transcendence from my childhood until now.

Frank MacEowen speaks beautifully of the journey of life as a mist-filled path. Many of us have experienced forests where the mist gently rises from the moss and undergrowth that is renewing the forest itself. For me, as for MacEowen, it is a reminder that in the mist lives sacred Celtic traditions and calls us to embrace the mist in our search for meaning. MacEowen recalls a special event in his life that altered his world. "On one day in particular when I was out in the trees, something happened. I had a sudden and shocking remembrance of the trees as guardians, allies, and as conduits for activating memory. Images flashed in my mind. The images were hauntingly familiar, achingly so. ...in that moment, the trees suddenly told me that they were my ancient home, that I had known them intimately before, and that one day I would live among them again. I was deeply stirred and in the midst of this experience I realized that the spirit of the mist did not retreat from my presence that day. It moved in around me, encompassing me like a cool blanket. Slowly I began to feel at one with the forest, at one with the mist, and at one with myself in a way I never had before. I was suddenly self-aware, profoundly conscious that life is a path that we walk from the time of birth to the time of death."[31] While perhaps not as dramatically, I, too, have experienced such a melding with the spirit of trees and the protection of the various guardian spirits of trees from my childhood through today.

Along with the Celts' honoring of trees, they also believed that all of nature, every aspect, every animal, every plant, and flower had a guardian spirit. The guardian spirit was often itself an animal. Ted

Andrews explains, "Nature spirits are those beings and spirits associated specifically with nature. Every society taught that there were spirits associated with everything growing upon the planet. Every tradition had its own way of naming these spirits. Nature spirits are Mother Earth's children. They are as many sided as Nature Herself, coming in a multitude of sizes, forms and degrees of development and creativity. Every flower has its fairy, every tree its spirit. There are unicorns and other fantastic creatures within the natural world as well."[32]

Freeman notes, "Despite the way the faery world has been banished to the hinterland of modern consciousness, the healing powers of the Otherworld have always been available to those who are called to become healers themselves...."[33] It does my heart good to know that others have had the privilege of meeting these fairy creatures who saved my psyche as a troubled and vulnerable child. Assurance that these entities which meant so much to me in childhood and throughout my devotion to nature are now available to me both as a healer and one who is on a healing path is even more precious.

The Celts believed that all of life moved in a motion that is spiraling in nature. I noticed as I studied Celtic traditions that I only needed to look at the expression of the Celtic Chakra system to see an immediate difference in perspective. It is an interesting alteration. Elen Sentier, prolific author in all things Celtic, describes the system as a spiraling system.[34] An explanation of the Celtic system is also found in an excerpt from her book. That excerpt appeared in *Daily Om*. It is quite consistent with the Celtic belief system and the concept of a spiraling journey. She describes the Celtic Chakra system, like many things Celtic as spiraling in nature. In explaining the spiral path, she refers to the triskele (three spirals connected to each other). She notes that it "spins and spirals its way through the Celtic chakra system".

While the traditional understanding of chakras forms a straight line from base to crown, Celts would understand this as representing simple linear time. The spiral, however, contains "both the cycles and the sense of progression but without the restricting points of continuous outward expansion or continual return to the same place. It is more in alignment with breathing and of both continuity and newness."

The ordering of the chakras when doing Celtic Chakra work is quite different from the usual linear approach. You begin at the heart center and then go down to the heart's partner, the solar plexus. From there you spiral up to the throat chakra and then go down to the sacral center just below the belly button. From the sacral center, you spiral up to the crown center. She warns against staying centered in the crown center as it is easy to drift away. At that point, you spiral down to the Base Center (the Root Center). From there you go up to the brow center. The brow center is the place where all the threads from the other six centers come together and are "integrated into a wholeness that is you in this lifetime."[35]

One only need look at the art of the Celts, both ancient and contemporary to see that the spiral symbol simply dominates all other attempts at art. Freeman explains, — "Everywhere we look, we see that life moves in a spiral motion. From snail shell to sunflower, from the invisible coils of the DNA molecule to the boundless whirling galaxies, life unfolds as a spiral. This simple pattern holds the secret to the whole universe, for within its form lies the feminine circle and the masculine line. Without these two....movements, there would be no motion and consequently no life in this world of opposites.... In Celtic countries people have danced in spiral since time began. Even today people of Brittany dance in all-night festivals where the music of bagpipe and hurdy-gurdy never stops. Slowly and rhythmically, they move into the center and out again in huge spirals."[36]

While I always understood that life 'worked' in a spiral, I had not applied it directly to my spiritual and emotional life. For example, throughout my life, I spiraled in and out of clarity. I followed the spiral path upward only to find that some unknown event or circumstance could send me back down the spiral to begin again. While frustrating, this spiraling motion gives me second and third and fourth chances to what I need to change to support those moments of insight and stability. There have been times on my journey when obstacles have almost completely blocked my way. I lost hope, ideas for new ways of doing deserted me. It seemed almost as if my personal Tree of Life had lost her leaves. I hit dead end after dead end unable to see the proverbial 'light in the tunnel'. I took wrong turns and felt as if I was going in circles arriving nowhere. And, at times, many times in fact, I have allowed my fear to get the better of me and did not grasp the lessons that are there for the taking. It is at such times that it becomes life-giving and life-saving for me to see the healing in the journey itself and to embrace the difficult path that lands me on the upward or inward spiral once more.

The Celts believed that there were three worlds to explore. There was the Underworld, often symbolized by the roots of the Tree of Life, the Upperworld or the branches, and the Middleworld—the world in which we live although perceived as a different reality. They speak of 'thin places' or places where one can step from one world into another. These places were often where there were caves or perhaps where the water met the land, at dawn or sunset, or where the roots of the trees met the earth from which they draw nourishment.

MacEowen speaks eloquently of thin places. "Thin places are potent doorways within our sacred world, which includes the natural world (and aspects of the human world) and domains that permeate and lie beneath our world. It is where the ordinary and non-ordinary come to rest in each other's arms. These places might be in-between places or particular in-between times, such as twilight. Celtic thin places are crossroads where the world of the spirits and the world of the embodied mingle. It is where the realm of human and faery touch. It is where living descendants and the ancestors commune. It is where the unseen and the seen share one ground…. It is where the ordinary and non-ordinary come to rest in each other's arms. … we align ourselves with what I call the shimmering peace of a place. We open ourselves to its mysteries… dialogue with the holy energies, with the spirits."[37] And, as I do so, I remember that I am Divine.

Thin places are also described as "Tween Times and Places". They are in-between this world and the other. "They are times and places where a thinning of the veils between the physical and spiritual worlds occurs. This thinning of the veils, these Tween Times and Places, makes us more sensitive to subtle things around us. They are doorways and windows through which we experience psychic, magical, and spiritual phenomena more clearly. And using this secret of Tween Times and Places is the key to actual spirit encounters."[38]

I believe that I have always been very aware of these thin places and have always looked for them. My special places have always been what I now can describe as 'thin places' and I suspect that because of my ability to see one world and live in another, the profound importance of these places may be one particularly important 'gift' of mental illness. I often feel as if I am living in two worlds at once and the thought of having one foot in one world and one foot in the other is so typical as to make it not frightening at all. I do not think that I ever actually viewed these worlds as distinct and separate. It was simply the way I lived.

It was exciting for me to realize that Celtic Spirituality welcomes my longing for a unique way of being in this world and encourages me to explore other worlds. What seem like magical creatures are part of another world which is difficult to see and understand at times. But now I do not feel 'out of touch' with reality when I experience these times, I, indeed, feel very much in touch with this special sense of the deeper workings of this world. This realization gives me a framework from which I can understand my sometimes spinning and spiraling moods. And my world is considerably less frightening than it was without that framework.

As the discussion of spirits and spirit guides unfolds it is important to remember and elevate the importance of Nature Spirits. Certainly, rich in the Celtic traditions, they also hold great meaning in other beliefs as well. According to Ted Andrews, "Nature spirits are those beings and spirits associated specifically with nature. Every society taught that there were spirits associated with everything growing upon the planet. Every tradition had its own way of naming these spirits. In the West, we most often refer to them as fairies and elves, but they have many more names. Nature spirits are Mother Earth's children They are as many sided as Nature Herself, coming in a multitude of sizes, forms and degrees of development and creativity. Every flower has its fairy, every tree its spirit."[39]

As I have relayed in the autobiographical section, fairies were my first spirit guides and guardians. They were all around me as I traveled through those early days, revealing themselves most often at the foot of a hill by a house that literally terrified me. They also lived under rocks, and flowers and toadstools. Their houses were in little indentations in the many trees in which I took comfort. They gave me almost the only escape I had from a world that was too difficult to bear for a three or four-year-old child. If I had grown up in Ireland, or any other Celtic country, my 'seeing' fairies would have seemed unremarkable. Celts believe that fairy people communicate with humans and humans go to great lengths to maintain good relationships with fairies and other Nature Spirits. I was ecstatic to discover the acceptance of this bonding with entities as completely 'normal' and even commonplace in other less rigid cultures. The folk spirituality that I experienced with fairies as a child and I now experience on a regular basis opens my heart to magic and new paths to community. This magical, mystical world brings me boundless joy in celebrating the vast creativity of Sacred Energy.

Now that I have broken free from the expectations that somehow told me to keep my fairies to myself, I regularly speak to them, even if I don't 'see' them as I walk the dog or take nature hikes. My camera is full of pictures of places in trees or undergrowth where I can imagine if not 'see' them living and hiding. I have one special fairy, Violet, who visits me every time I go to a historic site in Central Florida. She has unusual ways of showing me that she is there, even though I have only caught glimpses of her scampering off into the woods. For me, because of the long days of despair that I have encountered in my Bipolar experience, to embrace fairies and other mythical creatures is to return joy to my life—to return the childlike ability to believe in beings other than what my parents and teachers 'wanted' me to believe. When I say hello to the fairies every morning as I walk my dog, it gets my creative energies going and brings me pleasure. In a world where depression seeks to conquer hope, and anxiety deadens peace, the interaction with fairies and nature spirits is an exceptionally good thing indeed.

Celtic Spirituality integrates what I experienced with my longing to understand the sacred. It weaves together the worldly and other-worldly aspects of my life in ways that I can understand. And whether these mystical creatures are metaphorical or have physical form, they give me a sense of peace in both worlds. I understand that neither world is permanent; and, know that as I mature, I will become more comfortable in the 'world' in which I must exist in this moment.

14

Harmony and Balance: Native American Medicine

Although I have never had the opportunity to live and learn among a Native American tribe, their beliefs have always fascinated and comforted me. The emphasis on Nature and living in harmony with the earth has reinforced my desire to live balanced in nature and feel the stability that such balance brings. Native American scholar Michael Garrett notes, "Whatever lessons are most needed at the time emerge for the person as the spirit seeks to grow. As the elders would say, 'You have to sit with it…' Something like the love between Sun and Moon, for example, can be better understood as the natural harmony and balance that is needed for us to survive. It is an energy that exists in and of itself."[40]

For harmony and balance to exist, Garrett says there must be acceptance for things as they are. There it is again—acceptance. He talks of his own life, noting that while there are many things, he wishes he could change, he acknowledges the learning that took place with each event. He says, "I cannot go back and undo the threads of the past, and I would not want to…The self-destruction that occurs throughout guilt or blame takes one out of harmony and balance, though these things, too, offer important lessons."[41]

As I learn to live both with these things that I have done and the outcomes of consequences that occurred because of those events, I come to know that I can only be healed by what he calls the "Rule of Acceptance". He acknowledges he was sometimes left frustrated and wanting to know more about why things had happened. When Acceptance was all that surfaced in his quest, he began to understand that acceptance forces each of us to seek our own answers. I know many times I simply would not have been able to take on someone else's answers. Garrett says, "This is another important lesson of the Rule of Acceptance: Sometimes it is not the right answer that is important but asking the right question and being ready for whatever comes."[42] In fact, I know this happened to me on more than one occasion when a well-meaning friend tried to tell me what I was doing to get myself in trouble and I did not want to hear it. It was simply too soon for me to hear it, or I was in denial of the truth of the advice. He describes the role of Acceptance in life itself. "Understanding the flow of life allows us to let go of expectations, accept the limitations over which we have no control, and move with this flow. This way, we focus our 'Nuwati' (energies) on making intuitively informed choices about where our path is taking us and learn from the beauty of life—allowing our own spirit to flourish like a small wildflower opening its dewy petals to the bright and orangey morning sunlight. Expect nothing and appreciate the value of everything; this is the true lesson of the Rule of Acceptance."

As I think about acceptance, and my initial negative response, I am reminded to explore my constant need to control every situation in my life. This greatly contributed to my complete disintegration when the life I thought I was going to live spiraled far beyond my control. As soon as I began flailing against what was happening, I closed myself off to anything other than mere survival. Garrett points to another way. "The Rule of Acceptance teaches us about the importance of listening and opening up our spirits by giving away the need to control things, or change other people, or the need to control situations. These things remove us from the harmony and balance of the Circle, and just make life difficult when it does not have to be."[43]

Native American spirituality emphasizes balance. Balance, while I heard others speak of it, was almost non-existent in my life. I could not balance my life with my work, my diet with my lifestyle or my times of sane calmness with my times of spinning into manic places and relationships. Jim Pathway Ewing speaks profoundly of the Native American's purpose. While he may speak of it in the voice of Native American tradition, it makes sense to me as I contemplate my own life. He says, "It is our purpose, each of us, to bring balance to the Earthly Mother. In doing this, we bring balance to ourselves. ...that, then, is the aim, to bring our energies into balance. That is to recognize the Nuwati (Cherokee), the good medicine in all things. [In the] Native way the world outside reflects the world inside. They are one. But we don't try to manipulate the world to create inner states...that's backwards. We achieve an inner state and it reflects in the world, ever outward into The Sacred Hoop of Life where it is reflected back to us... The Great Secret is that we always carry The Sacred Hoop of Life within us all the time. It is up to us to use it, keep it whole. ...It is the soul connection that resides within each of us, the 'true' path we walk, that knows no time or place. For we carry it from lifetime to lifetime like underwater divers, their air hoses connecting them to above."[44]

The Sacred Hoop of Life is also explained as the Great Circle. Garrett points out that everything Native American is basically in the shape of a circle. Black Elk, Oglala Lakota Medicine Man, describes it as such. "You have noticed that everything an Indian does is in a circle, and that is because the Power of the World always works in circles, and everything tries to be round…The sky is round, and I have heard that Earth is round like a ball, and so are all the stars. The wind, in its greatest power, whirls. Birds make their nests in circles, for theirs is the same religion as ours…Even the seasons form a great circle in their changing, and always come back again to where they were. The life of a person is a circle from childhood to childhood, and so it is in everything where power moves."[45]

Staying in this never-ending circle keeps me in touch with the harmony and balance that comes from embracing a circle to describe life. A circle is not unlike a spiral, the metaphor I have used throughout this book. A spiral is simply a circle that descends and then ascends, but its basic form is circular indeed. As I have noted, things go awry when I step out of my spiral pathway, or, in this case, the sacred circle, and I lose the sense of harmony with life. For Native Americans 'Good Medicine' is described as being in alignment with the earth's sacred rhythms. If I move away from or step out of the circle, I find myself in a state of dis-ease which invites illness into my life. I am then out of balance and I cannot find the focus to reintegrate myself into the Great Circle. According to Jim Pathway Ewing, "We are each and all 'minute.' But the 'saving grace' is that we each have the power of the Creator within each and every one of us, which is greater than all. That is the power we access in giving our prayers. And that is the power we use to change our Dream of the World to bring balance to it. Balance is at the heart of the Flow of Creation."[46]

Living in balance is living in the presence of this 'Good Medicine'. But it does not guarantee a care-free, challenge-free life of ease. Indeed, just the opposite may be true. Garrett clarifies, "What it does mean is making constructive and creative choices through clear intention (wisdom) to fulfill one's purpose in the Greater Circle of Life by maintaining and contributing to the reciprocal balance of family, clan, tribe, and community in the context of personal, social, and natural environments."[47]

This is a difficult place to be. I want to believe that I will be able to make 'constructive and creative choices' and utilize the wisdom I have gained to become a part of the community, but my past decisions have not always been so great. This is a spiritual question, a crisis, regarding whether I can trust myself to change and whether I have a vital place in this world, a purpose, if you will. Since I cannot do this amid crisis, I must learn during my stable times how to move myself through whatever circumstances come my way.

There are days when even thinking about concepts such as harmony and balance is too difficult for me. So, I don't. Jamie Sams, in *Dancing the Dream*, talks about the meaning of times of desperation. Sams speaks of the 'Dark Nights of the Soul'. Like the words of the early Christian mystics, her explanation brings me hope. She says, "In our Native American tradition, we see the Dark Nights of the Soul as rites of passage, initiations that call us to respond in ways that ultimately temper and strengthen the warrior nature contained in the human spirit. Any woman or man or child on the earth can embrace that bravery within themselves, …experiencing a victory over the Dark Night of the Soul simply by surviving, knowing that they have done the best that they could at that time. Accepting these difficult rites of passage allows us to be brave, to take courage, and to acknowledge the warrior nature of our spiritual essences. The awakened human spirit walks the paths of human transformation with exacting grace and has been waiting for us to discover the power of the spiritual warrior existing inside us. If we act from our warrior nature, facing the issues at hand rather than shutting down during harrowing times, we will not have to repeat the difficult lessons that life uses to force us to confront unpleasant issues. Then we finally begin to understand the hidden strengths of our personal Medicines."[48]

I want to jump up and shout 'yes' when I hear such positive interpretations of these 'rites of passage' and her words cause me to sift through my own many dark nights and see the powerful transformations that emerged. I think I missed those transformations as they occurred because I expected them to be earth-shattering. Often, I know now, they may just have been the courage to get up and walk the dog.

Native Americans also have a sophisticated approach to the coherence of the mental and physical. In fact, there is no question but that the mental (or psychological) part of a person is integral to their understanding of the physical aspects. According to the Garretts—there is no difference and both parts are in unity. This lends great understanding to what I have learned about the physical/biological nature of mental illness. If there is unity, then illness in one part of the body is illness in both. Native Americans accept the use of medications and psycho-therapeutic interventions without judgment. The Rule of Acceptance as it is applied to others brings a special significance. "The answer is the traditional teaching of acceptance, showing respect and allowing dignity without criticism for anyone or any approach used that causes no harm and allows for healing within the person, including the family and the environment."[49]

With its emphasis on nature and energy, Native American thought begins to bring me to an understanding of 'Indian Medicine' that is profoundly similar to other forms of energy healing I have experienced. The Garretts define the word "spirit" to refer "to an active and alive flow of energy that connects us all in the Universal Spirit."[50] Healing energy is described as a "sense of calm that unblocks or harmonizes the vibrations or frequencies that are out of control."[51] "Early Cherokee 'helpers' would use noncontact ways to direct healing energy. They would warm their hands over a sacred fire. Then use circular motions about seven inches from the physical body to stir or unblock the natural energy. They would also hold the hands upward the sky and picture in their minds the person they were about to heal, then send the energy for healing.... The 'helpers' would also use contact ways such as touch—especially gentle pressure on key spots—to relieve pain and to enhance energy movement for the body to heal itself naturally."[52]

I have often felt solidarity with Native Americans and have read often of the 'Great Circle' in which they live and embrace all of life. I remember learning that Native American make decisions only after discussing how they will affect children seven generations out. I think of all the decisions I have made and the decisions made for and about me and know that this is a profound concept. I have driven through reservations in Florida, North Carolina, New Mexico, and Texas, and observed the abject poverty, but there is a spirit there that calls out to me to honor their perseverance and determination. It is a spirit that I feel in myself and it has served me well. As I look forward to exploring more into the study of Native American beliefs. I sense that there is much to mine there as I continue in my quest amid living with Mental Illness to find the fullest life possible.

Native Americans have shown me great love in my inner life. In my hikes and walks through the woods of at least five states over several decades, I have seen the shadowy spirits of ancient people whom I did not know. I see them off in the woods, sometimes we just exchange moments of looking into each other's eyes, but often they are going about their daily business of surviving. I believe that my anger about the theft of their lands may form a link between our spirits and help me work through my feelings of loss and homelessness. Whatever the case, it is their kindness in allowing me to 'visit' with them that reinforces my feelings of belonging. And the feeling of belonging may well be what is most important for me to experience since I have spent my life believing that I was an 'outsider'. Inclusion in the great tradition of oneness and the protection of Great Spirit, to walk in their presence full of history and deep, life-giving beliefs regarding the sanctity and preciousness of all life is a spiritual gift indeed and helps to mend my broken heart with gifts of love and compassion.

15

With a Beat of the Drum: Universal Shamanism

Many traditions speak of healers as 'wounded healers'. Shamanism refers to this type of wounding (crisis) as necessary for almost all Shamans except for those who inherit the role. As I have indicated several times, I believe myself to be such. As a wounded healer I have had many 'initiations' into the world of healing. However, I have come to view my most recent and intense episode as the one which spurred me into a profound search for meaning and spirituality—one which would change my life completely. This initiation, first into hopelessness, then into a greater search for understanding allowed me, for the first time in my life, to embrace the readiness to challenge myself, to transform and to find the healing energy that had been with me all along. I yearned for a more dynamic, more comprehensive, and life-giving understanding of my journey and mental illness in general. For me, though perhaps not for others, this required diagnosis and stabilization.

Even though I had not studied Shamanism before, I found myself strangely and strongly drawn to that system of beliefs. As I followed that intuitive call, I discovered I was particularly intrigued by the practices of Initiation, Journeying, Power Animals and Guides, and Soul Retrieval. These beliefs hidden deep in my unconscious surfaced as I sought the cohesion I was looking for. The combination of energy healing and Shamanic practices have led to a profound sense of integration to my thoughts and consciousness. I have explored this tradition (a collection of traditions from all over the world) as integral to understanding mental illness. In fact, in the Shamanic view, mental illness or psychosis often signals 'the birth of a healer'. Thus, mental disorders are spiritual emergencies, spiritual crises, and aid in the formation of the healer. This resonates with my self-understanding as a wounded healer and as a spiritual teacher. My study of Shamanism has led me to my most precious healers and helpers: my Spirit Guides, my power animal and the many who have gone before (my Circle of Guides) as they have played a significant role in my understanding of and embracing my mental illness. My inner conversations with each of them is an ongoing way for me to embrace their significance as I live all sides of mental illness and sacred transformation.

This description of Shamanism from Anne Dorian resonates with my experience. "Shamanism is a love story – this is about falling in love with yourself, life, and the raw, wild beauty of creation. Shamanism is native to all of us and is one of the oldest animistic traditions in our human heritage – we two leggeds have had some form of Shamanic practice in each of our ancestral cultures on planet earth since time began. ...Shamans served their community by working closely with helping spirits, and keeping their tribes or clans safe, healthy, happy and connected to the natural world."[53]

I first began to be fascinated by the study of Shamanism when I studied the role of Shamans and Druids in the Celtic tradition. Almost at once, I found myself drawn to Shamanic beliefs and practices as the single most important contribution to the integration of my mental illness in the context of my sacred transformation. I often look back and say to myself, you've come a long way in the 40 years since your ordination in 1978 as a Southern Baptist Minister to becoming a 'homegrown'[54] spirit-led Shamanic Practitioner. Congruent with the path I have journeyed, it is also the path that has brought understanding to my mental illness as well. I honestly believe that a different, perhaps less western culture would have seen my experience at 17 as my first call to the Shamanic life. I certainly understood the call to become a healer, but I did not know how to do that; and, no one around me had any guidance to give me on what for them was a 'troublesome' subject.

As I noted before, much of the lore and history of the Celtic peoples was denigrated by various invasions of Christians who outlawed so-called 'pagan' practices and tried to destroy what little history had been compiled. Nevertheless, because most Celtic history and mythology is recorded in songs and poetry, we do have much history to explore. In *Oak, Ash and Thorn*, one of the most thorough explorations of Celtic Shamanism, D. J. Conway suggests that most people think of Druids who had the "powers of healing and prophecy, and experienced great spiritual revelations"...This personal mystical practice is not categorized in the surviving Celtic accounts, but then so much was deliberately destroyed by the Christians that one cannot say what may or may not have been written about it.

However, there are enough descriptions of what certain people did, how they acted, and the powers they could call upon that there is little doubt as to what this practice was. It was a branch of European Shamanism... it became a crime to practice or teach Shamanism, as happened with many other Pagan beliefs. The only remaining descriptions of Celtic Shamanism are clothed in myths and legends.[55] What the invading Christians failed to realize or, more likely, chose to ignore is that Shamanism does not challenge any other belief and can, in fact, make other spiritual expressions more meaningful. When studied without prejudice, it becomes clear that there is no conflict.

As I studied Celtic Shamanism, I encountered other forms of Shamanism. The basic principles and even practices extend across continents, eras, and societal structures. The expression of such similarities may differ, but the basics are, for the most part, the same. Shamanism is not a doctrine; it is a way of living. Through Shamanic practices I learned to experience nature at her deepest reaches. As I studied and continue to study, Shamanism teaches me, in ways that demand complete alignment with all living things, exactly what I need to survive and my place in this incredibly mystical and magical world. It provides a path when I wander away from mine without demanding that I adhere to a certain set of beliefs. In yet another way, I learn to live harmoniously with all of creation. This alleviates any demand to pledge allegiance to any distinct way of experiencing the Sacred. The practice of Shamanism continues to lead me to an understanding of a connection between and among the twists and turns of my life. Shamanism not only encourages me to take responsibility for my own well-being; it requires that my personal work ultimately change the world.

Shamans recognize the close relationship with the powers of the Earth and Nature. They learn to use all those powers and sources of energy as they are gifted to them by animals, plants, and all living beings. Because special guides and spiritual helpers are often from the plant and animal world, this relationship with nature is particularly important. D.J. Conway notes, "often these powers are not what would be considered usual, they can appear in distinct types of energies and powers to each Shaman. Shamanism is one of the most individualistic of practices...The purpose of a Shaman's work today, as well as in the past, is to help others...by helping others transcend ordinary reality, the Shaman can help them transcend their pictures of themselves as sick or diseased. When the individual can do this, she/he knows from the results of the work that she/he has become a true Shaman."[56] John Matthews reminds us, "No Shaman walks alone. Each has his or her spiritual allies, who work alongside them and guide their steps. These allies may take the form of mythic heroes, divinities, spiritual leaders, or ancestors. Their task is to be companions, friends who travel along the many secret paths of the otherworld. They are there to act as wise advisors, making sure we follow the right path and travel with integrity and grace."[57]

In the preface to *Awakening to the Spirit World: The Shamanic Path of Direct Revelation,* Sandra Ingerman writes: "Shamanism reveals that we are part of Nature and one with all of life. It is understood that in the Shaman's worlds everything in existence has a spirit and is alive, and that the spiritual aspects of all of life are interconnected through what is often called the web of life. Since we are part of Nature, Nature itself becomes a helping spirit that has much to share with us about how to bring our lives back into harmony and balance. At the experiential center of Shamanism lies the potent path of direct revelation, revealing that in this spiritual discipline, there are no intermediaries standing between the helping spirits and ourselves. We all can have access to the wisdom, guidance, and healing that the helping spirits and Nature have to share with us."[58]

Shamans know that the wisdom or energy for their work does not come from themselves. Shamans never use their own energy. They are merely the conduit. Many times, they learn the work they are to undertake from their power animal. As Shamans do their work they rely on the power of the Universe. Villoldo, tells us that his journey into Shamanism "was guided by my desire to become whole. In healing my own soul wounds, I learned to love myself and others. I walked the path of the wounded healer and learned to transform the grief, pain, anger, and shame that lived within me into sources of strength and compassion."[59] While certainly true for me, I am also sure that many who come to Shamanism come by way of similar transformation. Shamanism is a way of life in which anyone can take part. It can enrich anyone's life who is willing to practice it with a sense of gratitude, awe, and the willingness to put study and reflection into one's practice. I can say without doubt that the combination of Shamanism and Reiki as healing methods has changed my life significantly since my diagnosis now several years ago. When I include the wonderful mystical nature of my Celtic background and the Native American emphasis on harmony and balance, I begin to grasp the spiraling nature of healing and life.

In *Awakening to the Spirit World*, referenced above, Hank Wesselman states his belief that "All true Shamans are gifted visionaries... Shamanism is the path of immediate and direct personal contact with Spirit, deeply intuitive, and not subject to definition, censorship, or judgment by others. On this path, each seeker has access to this transcendent connection and all that this provides."[60]

Out of respect for ancient Shamans and those indigenous Shamans of today, many people who during earlier times would have been considered a Shamans do not call themselves Shamans but rather Shamanic Practitioners. I use both designations to refer to myself though I make no pretense about having trained with an indigenous Shaman or traveled around the world participating in conferences and trainings. My financial situation and other limitations prevent me from training with an individual Shaman. Hence my 'home-grown' description. The journey to become a Shaman or Shamanic Practitioner has taken me over 60 years and my aptitude and insight continue to grow every day. Few believe that people choose to take part in Shamanic practices; they are called through a primal, life-altering event in their lives. Wesselman and most other scholars call this an 'initiation'. He states, "There are many experiences of initiation that may sculpt a person into a Shaman or a visionary. Typically, an individual in an indigenous community will have a psychological crisis or near-death experience, or they will be called by a voice from nowhere. Sometimes a person will have a visionary visit from a powerful spirit-being or ancestor in their dreams or endure a life-threatening illness or a psychotic break. With these experiences the initiate often achieves a momentary state of transcendence and experiences oneness and unity with the All..."[61]

Ingerman, also speaks of the formation of Shamans. She notes that most Shamans have experienced a near-death experience, a life-threatening illness, or a psychotic break; in her case it was an event of near drowning that opened her up to Shamanism. She states that "this near—death experience showed me the way to the other side. Shamans are those who have gone to 'the other side' and come back to life on their own, bringing back the knowledge of how to make the transition from life to death and then back to life again. In the Shamanic literature the term for this person is 'wounded healer'. A Shaman can help a dying soul who is lost or confused about how to make the transition by guiding the soul either to the light or to a deceased relative who will take it the rest of the way."[62]

Colleen Deatsman, in her book, *The Hollow Bone: A Field Guide to Shamanism*, elaborates on the nature of call. 'Psychological crisis, mental illnesses, and bouts of madness are, in many cases, signs—and sometime the hallmark of a Shamanic calling. These experiences are known to open the doors to the non-ordinary, spirit realms of energy and power in quick and extraordinary ways. Like Shamans who undergo physical illness and healing as their calling, Shamans who experience mental illness or madness are pulled immediately and spontaneously into the realms of spirit to sink or swim, so to speak."[63] In a culture where such initiations are accepted, there is a community of wise men and women who immediately undertake further training and teaching. Of course, I had no such community and was unable to process this for myself for almost 45 years.

And so, as I was trying to make sense of the breakdown that incapacitated me for a period of several months, I came to the question of how I was to use this experience to help others. Even as I was struggling with trying to figure out how I was going to go on in this life, I was also questioning in the furthest reaches of my mind what this would all mean. That part of my mind, I now know, is what kept me alive (even if I was rarely conscious of it). I could not and would not believe that my life had come to this end, and even in my absolute and total despair, there was a hidden spiritual knowledge that something bigger than my fight for survival was occurring. I did not speak of this to anyone; I barely spoke of anything. But my spirit was not extinguished although it may have looked so to others. Allowing the changes to take place is the very nature of the 'wounded healer' as it applies to Shamanism—and, quite frankly, as it applies to my life.

Scholars such as Dr. J.A. Kent have noted that Westerners (such as me) have a challenging time accepting, not only the initiatory experience but also the calling to recognize that one is a Shaman. He notes that most people go through a period "of ontological shock before getting to the stage where they could accept the experiences for what they were—real contact with the worlds of spirit. In traditional societies this experience would be accepted and honored; in Western society it was generally accepted reluctantly and with a lot of accompanying soul searching and self-doubt."[64]

When I began to study the nature of Shamanism, it was as if I was called to it, by forces larger than I. While it was not pleasant, I embraced the psychological, spiritual, and physical breakdown as one of my many initiatory experiences, although this one was undoubtably the most significant. As I stated earlier, I have been unable to study with a specific Shaman, so, I did the next best things. I read every book I could get my hands on and took as many on-line courses as I could afford. It was difficult for me to forgive myself for being in a situation which made it impossible for me to study in person, but I suspect that working through those feelings (and continuing to do so) is indeed, part of the healing itself. Indigenous scholar, Malidoma Patrice Somé places my experience into a context that opens my heart to further learning, "To be attracted to an ancient way of life is to initiate one's personal spiritual emancipation."[65]

I believe that I am called to use these methods in my healing practice, and I will be guided as I need to be guided and ways will open for me to learn what I need to learn. According to Alberto Villoldo," Shamanic training often follows the path known to the Greeks of old as the 'journey of the wounded healer'—during which, the Shaman developed his or her powers and abilities as they self-healed. I believe that it is essential for me to experience significant healing before I can begin to do deeper Shamanic work with others. But the Shaman is different from the mystic, who can also go through a process of healing and discovery of the invisible world of energy and spirits."[66] Again, the difference between 'curing' and 'healing' becomes important. While

Shamans do sometimes 'cure' illnesses and injuries, their major work comes in supplying ways for people, communities, and the earth to become whole.

It is exceedingly difficult in a short space to supply enough information about Shamanism for a full understanding. Most importantly, the concept of three worlds are crucial in the tradition: the Upper World, Middle World, and Lower World. According to Sandra Ingerman, "The Upper World is experienced by some as ethereal.... In the Upper World I know that I am standing on something but am often unsure what is holding me there. Power animals can live here as well as teachers in human form who can offer wise guidance on human relationships.

In sharp contrast to the noncorporeal Upper World, the Lower World is reached through a tunnel leading down into the earth. Although nonordinary beings and occurrences are the rule here, the landscapes are often recognizably earth: caves, seas, dense jungle, and forests. I can stick my fingers into the earth here. The beings inhabiting the Lower World are the spirits of plants and animals, as well as human spirits who relate to the mysteries of the earth. Power Animals are often found here. The Middle World is recognizable as our own biosphere but transposed into a nonordinary key. In the Middle World the Shaman can travel back and forth through human histories. Sometimes the soul of a client has remained in a past moment of his or her life while the outer world has continued to move onward. To rescue such a soul, the Shaman must travel through the Middle World to this encapsulated moment and then find a way to get the soul out of it."[67]

Of equal importance is the belief in the existence of Helping Spirits. There are three most common types of Helping Spirits who work with the Shaman and aid in healing. First is the power animal.

This is not 'a' power animal but an entire species of animals, such as all lions, all ravens, all bears. No animal is better or preferred than the other. Spirit knows which animal each healer needs. There are also spirit animals who appear as they are needed. I did not choose my power animals. They chose me because I have many things to learn from them. Part of my journey toward becoming fully human then is the ability to value and respect the companionship of animals and my own responsibility to care for all animals in the process.

Trees and plants are also seen as spirits who are helpful in the Shaman's healing work. Teachers who can appear to the Shaman as human beings are often guides. These helping spirits act as intermediaries between us and the power of the universe. Their compassion for our pain, suffering, and lack of understanding, cause them to be ready to help. "These spirits could be called archetypal forces or even transpersonal forces that are ancient human experiences, and as the Shaman/visionary journeys back and forth between this world and these numinous realms, he or she gains access to different helping spirits on the diverse levels of the Lower and Upper Worlds. Through direct experience, the visionary learns where and to whom to go to for different types of help, yet, …It may be that the various helping spirits are all part of one source."[68]

My power animal (Turtle) gives me the wisdom, courage, and power to undertake all of life, and in this context, to share these deeply personal and until now private experiences and perceptions that I have recorded in this book. I am grateful for all that Turtle teaches me and the protection that Turtle gives me on my Shamanic journeys and in my life. Just as an example of the various attributes that power animals can possess, Turtle is a slow-moving creature (something which greatly helps me when I find myself moving into a chaotic manic state where my thoughts run wild and I long for quiet). Turtle always carries its own protection and I am therefore reminded to stay close to the earth and remain fully grounded. For me, as a person who lived much of my life feeling as if I had no protection, spiritual or otherwise, Turtle has much to teach me and, in doing so, shows me the way to safety.

R.J. Stewart, in his article, "Spiritual Animals, Guardians, Guides and Other Places", suggests that "certain individuals are naturally attuned to certain creatures, some animals or birds are more or less permanently attuned, while others work for specific phases of a lifetime. If we are able to find these creatures, many of our individual energies are greatly enhanced, and in many cases, rebalanced harmoniously in areas that were previously weak or out-of-tune."[69] When I first began my work in Shamanic practices, a silver horse with a long mane that flowed as she ran showed up in my dreams and forest walks quite often. I finally came to realize that she was sent to show me that I was on the path of freedom and that I was free to 'fly' through the work ahead. Occasionally, she returns, but her work in my life seems finished for this present time. The other animal that appeared was an owl, always white, always high in a tree. While she was the bearer of wisdom, I think she was also the presence of my mother (who collected owls all her adult life). I did not feel any judgment or positive energy from her. It was just as if she were watching, just waiting to see where this would all go. Perhaps the need for a mother to watch over her child truly never ends and she was present to continue that task. I hear her singing lullabies at times, and they comfort me when I am particularly anxious.

As I was studying more Shamanic practices, I felt that it was the right time for me to seek my Shamanic Spirit Guide. It is frequent practice for Shamans to always have their Power Animal accompany them on journeys, and so Turtle was there as I began my journey. In

Shamanism, the Underworld is the realm where Spirit Guides live. I began in my usual quiet and safe place at the base of my trusted Spirit Tree and this time crossed over the stream. Not far from the stream was the same tree I have seen many times with an entrance near where the roots rise above the ground. I descended this tunnel (I would come to make this journey down this tunnel many times) and found myself in a lush forest. Most of the trees were like pine and birch trees situated far apart with a great deal of groundcover in between them. Turtle was comfortably gliding through the groundcover; I stumbled on vines a few times, but we walked in silence for a while. When we reached a clearing, I asked that my Spirit Guide appear. Several spirits in human form (at least I saw them in human form) appeared but each one told me that they were not my spirit guides. Finally, a cloaked figure appeared and informed me that they were my Spirit Guide. During this journey, I began to ask questions of my Guide and knew that I was beginning a wonderful, ever deepening relationship. While Spirit Guides have no need for human form, I suppose I have a need to visualize in such a manner. Therefore, when I envision my Spirit Guides, they are almost always a brown-cloaked figure with no indication of gender although I sense a feminine presence. I learned in that moment that I could refer to them as Maralda. As far as any relevant meaning attached to the name, I later learned that Maralda is a shortened form of the name Esmeralda related to the word 'emerald'. This bright green gem often represents the Heart Chakra and it does not surprise me that Maralda reminds me often to 'go with my heart' since my heart has been so bruised and broken over time.

Maralda is both my Guide and Teacher. I refer to Maralda as 'they' because they are a host of guides and teachers, but it is easier for me to conceive of them in the form of a single entity. I often receive brief teachings and sometimes, I share those teachings with others as part of my healing work. However, their teachings and guidance about my daily practice are almost constant and complex and relate to my work in healing and teaching. I do not always react well to their instruction, but I have come to know that their only motive is to further my highest good and the highest good for those with whom I come in contact. They along with Turtle give me the wisdom, courage, and power to undertake all of life, and in this context (drafting this book), to share this deeply personal story.

I began to discover that Maralda and Turtle had always played a role in my life, but I had no way to recognize them or acknowledge them. Turtles have always been one of my favorite creatures and, interestingly (or weirdly) enough, I spent two years in junior high school running extremely humane (and later useless) experiments with the turtles you could then buy in dime stores. My turtles received royal treatment and 'experiments' focused on the color of water preferred by turtles. I developed many ways to 'measure' the effects of color on turtles. I won several prizes from my projects though it was later determined that turtles are color blind. Just for the record, I don't believe my turtles or other turtles are color blind at all, but I let the adults in my life believe what they needed to believe. What I do believe is that turtles respond to the vibrations of certain colors so that even if they could not 'see' that the water they were swimming in was colored red, they were able to feel the vibration associated with that color and experience whatever impact those vibrations had on their behavior. Strangely enough, the turtles seemed to have favorite 'colors' and they were not always the same. While running the 'experiments' I spent numerous hours talking with them and we developed quite a bond. Thankfully, buying turtles at dime stores became outlawed because of abuses by stores and by consumers but my turtles were well cared for until they died natural deaths.

As for Maralda, I saw them off and on throughout my life, but always dismissed their presence as a shadow on the wall or a shift in sunlight in the forest. Nevertheless, when I finally met them in journey, I had the sense that they had been with me for a long time. I suspect, though I cannot prove it, they were there with me in the darkest of my nights throughout my entire life when I did not know how to go on. I believe they sat with me and made it possible for me to sleep.

My other Spirit Guides, who revealed their name to be Ciorcal (the Celtic word for circle) came to me quite unbidden, but at a time when I greatly needed them. I suspect at that time, early in my journey back from disintegration, I had no idea of what I needed at all. I am certain that these circles of light which surround me with a human-like presence and energy are the spirits of those who entered a higher level of consciousness and transition from this world to the next because of a successful suicide experience. They are with me constantly. Sometimes I feel as if Ciorcal has melded with my aura, they feel so close to me. They seem determined to keep me on my feet and moving forward even when it might be easier to choose to surrender to my mental illness. And by that, I don't necessarily mean suicide (anymore) but rather the demanding work of staying afloat when a sea of depression hits or giving in to the constant taunts of anxiety and return to disintegration.

The experience of interaction with my Spirit Guides and Power Animal is crucial to my understanding of the interweaving of spirituality and mental illness throughout my life. I have always felt completely and terribly alone. Deep inside, I knew there were others there, but I received no encouragement in retrieving those helpers or even talking about them. So, while I knew they were there or suspected as much, my desire to appear less crazy than I knew I already appeared kept me from asking questions or allowing any of the professionals with whom I worked to have even an inkling that I was battling the desire to share the reality of these guardians with anyone. It only made sense to me that someone had to be guarding me or I would have been 'gone', in one way or another, from this daily struggle long before my sixth decade.

I am sure that the early prohibitions against anything paranormal, or that harkened of the 'occult' was a major factor in keeping me silent. But it was very much the fear of the reaction of those whom I might tell that denied me the opportunity to speak my truth. I tried extremely hard to put all these experiences in a neat box, tie it up and label it 'God' but that really didn't work all that well for me. My inner world was in conflict with the outer world. This is not altogether negative. While constrained from telling anyone of my 'secret' experiences, I was, nevertheless, continuing, on an unconscious level to develop a relationship with all these guardians and helpers.

I believe one of the things that happened for me in my psychic and physical disintegration was that, because I was so desperate to live, my heart began to break open and allow all these other realities to slowly emerge from the hiding places upon which we had mutually agreed. I found this to be true in the writings of many people. People who have denied themselves full access to the divine within because it did not look like everyone else's require the tools of time, brokenness, despair, and finally, hope, to allow them to surface to full and higher consciousness.

Mike Williams in *Follow the Shaman's Call* describes my reality succinctly. "Shamans seem to be different from other people. They regularly cross the portal connecting this world to the otherworlds and, in a sense, live on the boundary between the two. Today, mainstream society shuns those who do not fit in and marginalizes their existence and yet, in Shamanic communities, these are exactly the people who are recognized and celebrated for the gifts they have been given."[70] I don't think that I ever (and certainly do not now) expected to be recognized or celebrated, I just longed for acceptance. Understanding the nature of my true call has helped me come to terms with the loneliness, isolation, and lack of understanding I endured much earlier in my life.

Shamans journey on behalf of the person needing healing or on behalf of herself/himself for many different purposes. Sometimes it is to meet and bring back a person's power animal or spirit guide(s). There are other journeys as well. These words from *By Ash, Oak, and Thorn* hold the greatest lesson that any healer, Shamanic or not, must learn. "Before you can use your Shamanic methods to help others, you must be able to help yourself. A Shaman must empower her/himself by identifying and dealing with past events that are still affecting this life. She/he must strengthen that empowerment by working with light centers and making certain that energy bodies are correctly aligned. This does not mean the Shaman will not experience illness, unhappy events, or discouragement. However, to minimize the negative effects of certain experiences, the Shaman must be personally aware of what is going on within her/his own body and mind."[71]

Shamans must use Shamanic practices to stay centered and balanced if they are to impact the world and bring healing to others. This requires much self-reflection and changes in priorities. Shamans must be willing to walk away from certain negative environments and embrace those which bring Light and Compassion into their souls. Shamans must undertake their own Otherworld journeys many times before she or he is able to help others take similar journeys. That crucial knowledge and skills gained in those journeys are found only in the Otherworld. Shamans cannot exist as Shamans unless they are willing to journey themselves and journey often. "It is soul, not spirit, that is the true landscape of Shamanism—the landscape of suffering, passion, and mess. Shamans deal with sickness, envy, malice, conflict, bad luck, hatred, despair, and death. Indeed, the purpose of the Shaman is to dwell in the valley of the soul—to heal what has been broken in the body and the community. Shamans live with betrayal, loss, confusion, need, and failure—including their own."[72]

There are many descriptions of the way Shamans work. Throughout my own work, several concepts are crucial. Shamans live in a world of perpetual gratitude. It is this gratitude that allows access to the spirit world itself. This humble thanksgiving (and one can see this throughout the history of Shamanism) opens the heart of the Shaman to enter a reality that brings healing, knowledge, and oneness. Shamans are also gifted with the ability to see things that others cannot. When Shamans have done their own work and are free of the bounds of ego and worldly limitations and expectations, they are able to tune into Spirit. Compassion arises, and the Shaman is able to help others. Shamans can see the totality of creation in a way that does not separate certain activities or conditions from others. There is a Life Force, a creative energy that flows throughout all that is. To be a Shaman is to understand power and the amazing things Shamans can do when they are whole themselves.

Perhaps the most crucial aspect of Shamanism for an alternative understanding of mental illness is 'soul retrieval' which is often referred to as 'soul-loss'. There are several ways to understand soul retrieval. What matters is that the part of the soul has broken off—probably years earlier, is returned or retrieved through a Shamanic journey and then returned to the soul of the participant thereby helping to make the participant whole (I, for one, had or have several parts of my soul which needed or needs retrieval). Contemporary psychology has adopted this concept although the vocabulary and 'treatment' is quite different. In my own experience words such as dissociation or Post Traumatic Stress Disorder may well refer to similar conditions. We know that the precise nomenclature is unimportant. A person who feels 'split off' from various 'parts' of themselves will find themselves unable to experience a fullness of energy or meaning.

In some ways, this soul part is in exile. This exile is painful no matter how it is described. I think I have almost always known of the 'soul loss' that occurred for me during my childhood. There were large parts of my childhood that I could not remember, and much of what I could remember was unpleasant and scary. I remembered good things like churning ice cream at my grandparents' house and playing with my cousins; but, much of the rest of it was simply missing. It also never occurred to me that later events (even into adulthood) also took with them pieces of my soul, which I needed to find and reclaim as my own. What I knew for sure is that the loss of these missing parts had a negative effect on any spiritual understanding of the depression and anxiety from which I suffered, because so much of my life was missing and I couldn't make it all 'fit'. So, once again, I did not feel 'enough'.

Sandra Ingerman notes that in the experience of trauma, "a part of our vital essence separates from us in order to survive the experience by escaping the full impact of the pain…Often when we give away our power, we become ill. Because the universe cannot stand a void, if we are missing pieces of ourselves, an illness might fill in that place." [73] Additionally, Caitlín Matthews in *Singing the Soul Back Home* speaks words that mirror my reality of soul loss. "One of the problematic aspects of soul-loss is that when human beings lose a vital part of themselves, they resort to other substitutes to 'fill the gap'. This is often the underlying cause of addictions. Soul-loss compounds emotional and physical diseases and is often at the heart of many long-term problems that have been submitted to various therapies which have been unable to bring anything more than slight alleviation. The reason for this failure becomes obvious if we understand the concept of soul-loss, since it is impossible to heal something which is not present... The concept of soul-loss clearly defines feeling and intuitions about ourselves which we've been hitherto unable to put a name to our trouble. Soul-retrieval restores the vital energy or 'will to live' without which therapeutic healing is useless."[74]

My own experiences and study led me to value greatly the work of Shamans throughout history and those who practice Shamanism today. The belief in soul retrieval resonated more with me than any psycho-therapeutic intervention I had previously experienced, even though there are similarities which are obvious though approached quite differently. From my perspective, psycho-therapeutic intervention seemed to focus on discovering how a 'part' went missing rather than re-integrating it. Soul retrieval can happen in journeying in two ways. In some cases, the person can set an intention and journey alone (with spirit helpers) to the place where the missing soul part sits in hiding waiting for reunification with the body from which it has fled. In the other case, the Shaman him/herself journeys for the person and brings back the part of the soul that needs retrieval and places it in the person in a ceremonial fashion. Both types are valuable and if one does not have access to in-person soul retrieval, other methods work with the setting of intention and willingness and wisdom to journey. In my experience, it is preferable to do this in the presence of a Shamanic practitioner. What follows is one of my most significant Shamanic journeys which led to an extensive experience of soul retrieval.

I attended a presentation by Kathryn Skaggs, Shaman, visionary, artist, and healer who said, among many things that "sometimes illnesses are just part of the plan"—for example, dementia may be a way of transition. In a statement which resonated with me greatly she suggested that sometimes people have illness to teach them something about themselves or to be able to give to and understand others.[75]

In my case, I set the intention to find out if there was soul loss associated with my father's abuse and the constant fear about his rages throughout my childhood. Now I had done hundreds of hours of traditional talk therapy along with some hypnosis therapy; but I never quite felt like I had reached the depth of my loss nor did I feel that I had become whole. This was a solitary journey. Kathryn led us through our journey with only the beating of the drum after giving us directions for entering the lower world. My power animal (Turtle) and my spirit guides Maralda and Ciorcal, traveled with me. While Turtle went with me as power animals always do, it was Ciorcal that I felt wrapping me in a protective shell as well as many other unidentified guides. I felt safe and unafraid.

The drumming started. I began my journey in my 'safe place'. Although it has grown in detail and beauty, it has, in some form or another, been the place where I would go in my mind anytime I desired safety, peace, or comfort for over 40 years. There is a large tree (my Tree of Life), with a comfortable place to sit now hollowed out among the roots of this great tree from my years of sitting up against it. There is a brook in front of me which I have used for decades in my meditative practice to focus on the leaves that floated by. Interestingly, much earlier in life, I built little nests for each of my 'parts' that I felt were 'missing'. This inner 'thin place' is now my place of departure for most of my journeys and with each journey it grows in beauty and detail.

I began by crossing over the small stream on stepping stones which helped make the miniature waterfalls in the stream itself. When I was on the other side, I journeyed down a path a short way when I came to a smaller tree which had a rather large hole at the base of the tree. As that deep hole drew me to it, I had no idea how I was going to enter it, but I instinctively knew that this was my portal to the Underworld for this journey. I dove in head first and righted myself as there was suddenly a tunnel tall enough for me to stand. I journeyed down the tunnel which had a rather steep descent but, again, I did not feel afraid. I felt Ciorcal almost lining the walls as I walked or floated down. When I arrived at the end of the tunnel, I stepped out into the lushest green mossy forest I had ever seen. The moss and ferns were everywhere creating a carpet of hundreds of colors of green. I instantly thought of my heart (the color green) chakra and knew of its broken-ness throughout my life. Animals walked along beside me, although no spirit in human form was present at this point. I did not see Turtle or Maralda, but I knew they were there watching and protecting me.

I came upon a clearing and there I could see a hologram of the house in which I had lived (and suffered the most abuse). I knew that it wasn't real and that I would not be able to touch it. I walked over closer and because it was not a physical presence, I was not fearful. I walked over to the place where the fairies had lived when I was a child and called to them. They appeared and seemed happy to see me. I turned and there was my dog Holly. She was my protector and she had died when I was five or six. She laid down on her side and invited me to lay down beside her and 'spoon' with her. I lay up against her, my head on her front leg and her back legs curled around me. I don't know how long I laid there feeling my breath in time with hers taking in her assurance that I was safe and need never be afraid again. I felt primal energy moving between us. She eventually stirred, and I got up. She assured me that anytime I was anxious or feeling manic, I could return to the feeling I had in her cuddle. I thanked her and kissed her and knew that I would see her many times again. I cannot explain my feelings except that I felt as though she had returned something valuable to me. Though not a true power animal, she was and is certainly a spiritual ally and I expect to see her again.

As I turned to go, I had the sensation of energy filling my first and second chakras. At first it was gentle, then it became more forceful and while it did not hurt, the pressure was quite extreme. With each push, even though it was uncomfortable, I felt more grounded. I was not afraid, though I was amazed at the physical sensations I was experiencing. Finally, the space in my body that housed the two lower chakras was filled and I turned to go. For the first time in my life, I felt my feet firmly against the earth and the fullness of energy radiated in my lower two chakras.

I felt the drumming change to call me home. And I began the ascent up the tunnel. I felt Ciorcal with me again, whisking me up the tunnel in time with the drum. When I emerged from the tunnel, I crossed over the stream and was fully present. Although I felt fatigued, I was in awe of what had happened. I intuitively knew that the soul part that had gone into hiding in that house was fully back inside me, filling my two lowest chakras with what they needed to balance and support me. To be honest, I felt a little shook up, but knew that with some meditation and rest I would be fine. I share this deeply personal journey of soul retrieval with you to let you know that this is real to me and that I believe with all my heart that the journey I took in 30 minutes (it felt like 3 hours) accomplished something that I had been unable to accomplish in therapy for more than a decade. In the telling of my journey and in the reliving of it, I feel even more healed by the events in the journey. I can also tell you that I have used Holly's invitation to lie up against her more than once in my battle with anxiety.

In an on-line presentation on Shamanism and soul retrieval, Sandra Ingerman talks about trauma as a "gift [that] comes from experiences that bring us to our knees". She speaks of how Shamanism saved her own life. Her question "How do I walk myself out of the darkness?" led her to study the 100,000 years of Shamanism that has worked with all kinds and levels of trauma. Trauma creates a "growth experience" although it could not have been possible for me to understand that at the time. Ingerman notes that we are born with a compassionate spirit who is a divine force who will circle around us and protect us. They will not protect us from growth; however, they will be there to observe and provide safety.

During trauma, she reminds us, the soul, or parts of the soul go into hiding, to protect us from the trauma itself. Sometimes a person can journey for themselves to retrieve a soul part but there are times when this requires the gift of the Shaman to travel into unknown realms to bring back healing spirits to help with the soul retrieval. As the life force that exists within, it is imperative that the soul must be whole. If parts of the soul are "lost", then power is lost as well. But after healing, the soul is pure light with creative energy to share.

Sandra Ingerman views trauma as an initiatory event. She acknowledges that she has been suicidal most of her life. She believes that the strength of spirit brought her through. She suggests that the most important thing one can do is to re-define trauma and to see it as a gift. And there are gifts of tools—tools that are useful in self-healing and those meant for my work with others. Shamans look at unseen energy, energy that others cannot see.[76] Even in the midst of trauma or healing from it, my spirit instinctively knows the way home and the Universe uses the trauma to bring me closer to the fire of compassion and healing.

Howard G. Charing, in his book, *The Accidental Shaman*, speaks about the keys of transformation. He lists three: intention, trust, and attention. INTENTION—all actions begin with an intention, a desire for a specific outcome. …while engaging in a Shamanic healing ceremony or healing practice, you need to know what you want to accomplish or where you want to go. TRUST—Gaining trust is an ongoing series of actions, feedback, and validation. 'Trust but verify' is a good practice to live by, and when you share your perceptions with another person, ask for feedback that will let you know whether you are on the right track. ATTENTION—Energy flows where attention goes. This principle addresses applying and focusing one's energy and intention.[77]

Though I could not have named what I needed as 'soul retrieval' I do not remember a time when I did not feel that something or someone was missing from my life. My earlier, rather radical attempts to find those 'missing parts' by engaging in an experiment with dissociative identity disorder shows me now, in the present, just how desperately I was looking for those 'parts' so that I could feel whole. I believe that as I journey for soul retrieval, over time, I will reach that gift of complete wholeness at least through the present. Obviously, additional trauma could cause another 'part' of my soul to go into hiding but it seems likely that these skills would help me identify and retrieve that part much sooner than in the past.

The Shamanic concept of soul loss is profound. Highly esteemed Shaman and scholar Alberto Villoldo says, "When a child is abused or traumatized, a fragment of his soul breaks off and returns to the archetypal domain of the Great Mother for the protection that his biological mother could not provide. This soul part is actually a portion of life energy that's now unavailable for his growth."[78] Bringing back this soul part is not a painless process as shown in my first journey. There are often tears and anguish in the returning of these missing soul parts and sometimes great regret. Yet my soul, when I trust it, knows what it needs to break free of the prison of incompleteness. These parts of the soul who have chosen, in their innate wisdom, to leave and hide when trauma happened in my life will come 'home' when I work to insure safety in the process of seeking wholeness. Soul loss can occur at any point in a person's life well beyond childhood. Soldiers in combat or people in accidents often experience soul loss. Intense grief can create soul loss when the spirit cannot bear the pain of the moment.

It is well known among Shamans that one cannot engage in soul retrieval for another person, until the Shaman has completed the full retrieval of his or her own soul loss. If my own story consumes my thinking and feeling; it is difficult to view others' stories through an objective lens. And while this is true in all the healing modalities, it is especially true in the ceremony of Soul Retrieval. Being 'stuck' in portions of my own story limits my ability to help others freely and authentically. Though my potential is limitless, this would place limitations on my abilities. By doing the arduous work of Soul Retrieval for myself I find freedom from my own story and make it so that I can be free to focus on the person in front of me. I am a wounded healer and doing my own work is the only way I can be of service to others. My scars and memories gift me with compassion for others and generates a passion to use all my woundedness in the service of others and for Mother Earth herself. Shamans are used by Source to heal others because they are fully present, fully familiar with their rich inner world and fully committed to the health and well-being of others. Shamans light up the world with their peace and grace as they continue to walk the way of the wounded healer.

As a wounded healer, I take great comfort and power in understanding the Shaman's task of becoming whole. It challenges me to look for and examine those parts of my soul that I have lost through the years of trauma through which I have lived. It encourages me to undertake necessary journeys to retrieve those missing parts of my soul and embrace my wholeness. The nature of the work of a wounded healer tells me that I am on the right path, engaged in the right work, and devoted to my highest calling.

16

Spiral Singing Tree: Spirit, Healing and Wholeness

As my work progressed it became obvious that I was beginning to create a healing 'system' that combines at least four of the traditions that had become invaluable in my own healing. Because combining more than one tradition can only enhance the healing experience for self and others, I developed a special interest in combining those systems into a multi-faceted personal system I began to refer to as Spiral Singing Tree. The realms of healing in Shamanism, the pouring out of healing in Reiki, the spiraling Celtic system of approaching the work of chakras in our overall health, and the Native American concept of harmony and balance all began to fuse together for me. Although this melding of practices is not original to me, it may be somewhat distinctive in my focus on the inter-weavings of mental illness and spiritual journey.

Osho talks about this journey. "The function of the healer is to reconnect, but when I say the function of the healer is to reconnect,

I don't mean that the healer has to do something. The healer is just a function. The doer is life itself, the whole."[79]

The use of the phrase Spiral Singing Tree is a way to constantly remind myself of the joining together of four forms of beliefs and energy healing with which I most identify—the Celtic forest alive with Nature Spirits and worlds waiting to be explored, Energy Healing in the form of Reiki bursting with renewal from the Universal Source, the harmony and balance of Native American peoples and Shamanism bringing its ancient methods of healing to a waiting world. Why Spiral Singing Tree? I believe that all the Universe vibrates with Cosmic Energy and the vibrational waves sing to our hearts, our cells, and our spirits. If we separate ourselves from the Earth, we will not be whole, healthy, or authentic. All these traditions insist on grounding in the reality of the sacred land on which we live.

The meaning of 'healer' and 'healing' has remained significant throughout the telling of my journey. Healing is, more than anything, related to making 'whole'. Celtic scholar Elen Sentier, quoted earlier, speaks about healing, "…It's very much about making whole, bringing together, synthesis, fusion. Curing is not really what constitutes healing or…the concept of 'put back together' particularly because of the word 'back'. There is no return, you can never go back to what was only something that looks similar to what you remember; the way, the path, is always forward, onwards. The path forward builds on the way we have already gone, the past is the rock on which we build the future…Healing in this way is about putting things together and about finding the roots of things… It's about consciousness, the centre of knowing…It is very much about the collecting, inward, centripetal energy that draws all things inwards to itself to bring them together, making whole from the outside in…"[80] As I contemplated the spiraling nature of healing itself, I began to understand that I was not looking for a 'cure' even if others were. My journey is mine alone, determined by Spirit working in and through me, expressing itself in a distinctive process. In mental illness as in all of life, we not only spiral 'down' into the depths of life, we also spiral 'up' into the heights of insight and higher consciousness.

Dianne Connelly, whose writing has influenced my thinking about the nature of healing gives me this beautiful insight: "The embrace, the perpetual taking of one's life in one's arms no matter what it looks like, the reconciliation of all the parts into one whole, the homecoming, the union of the personal with the cosmic…The call to life is from Life itself, our ground of being. Life is who we are. We are more than beckoned. We are summoned to embrace it as it shows up in our individual self, our community self, our global self. Together we receive the global clarion. Together we respond to the call and thus it is we who lead each other home."[81]

In my finding my way home, I received different gifts from each tradition. From Celtic wisdom I learned that I am both called and caller—that I seek and am sought. This became an overlay of my understanding of the calling of Universal Energy or Life Force. I did not think that I was worthy enough to call to Spirit. I certainly did not feel worthy enough to suspect that I was receiving a calling from Spirit or Source. Celtic thought taught me that I was both yearning for and yearned for in sacred transformation. An understanding of the Celtic Chakra system also gave me a new and different understanding of the flow of energies in our bodies and influenced the methods I use for Chakra Balancing or clearing.

As for specific healing traditions, I have found that the most important methods of both finding home and calling others home have been Reiki and Shamanism. I have known and practiced Reiki both before my diagnosis and since my reintegration. As I became more and more in touch with the healing nature of Shamanic practices and began to use them on myself, often in conjunction with performing self-reiki, I understood I had found a healing pathway that would greatly impact my own healing practices and my self-healing as well. The Native American beliefs which lead me to seek harmony and balance in my own life and healing brought a calming, embracing coherence to my healing practices. Because we humans love to name things, I struggled with what to call this combining of these four paths. I journeyed to visit with my guides and other spirit helpers with several questions. One of these questions, of course, was what to call this path that I had begun to work out for myself. The designation 'Spiral Singing Tree' seemed to resonate with all that I had discovered. One brief look at the internet will show hundreds of ways that practitioners combine Reiki and Shamanism—many of which are quite fascinating and informative. So, I do not, in any way, claim these thoughts to be original or unique. Wisdom, while happened upon or searched for in distinctively personal ways, always returns us to the great Source of Wisdom that has been ours to draw on all along.

While not exclusively Shamanic or Reiki in practice, Spiral Singing Tree uses the power of Reiki in traditional ways such as healing, relaxation, and general well-being. In and of itself, it is a wonderful expression of the presence of Universal Energy in all of us not unlike 'Nuwati' in the Native American tradition. In my Reiki and Shamanic work, I have come to realize that Reiki, for those who desire it, can also be a gateway to Shamanic Journeying and other Shamanic ceremonies. There is a commonly held belief that the founder of Reiki, Mikao Usui, was more than likely a Shaman as shown in his usage of the concept of the 'hollow bone' or 'hollow tube' through which Universal Energy flows. It can also be extremely helpful in self-healing and journeying for additional healing or insight. His use of sacred symbols also speaks of his connection to Shamanic practices. Reiki practitioners often sense that illnesses or imbalances are a result of lost parts of the self or from conditions from previous lifetimes.

Shamanism is among the most effective methods of identifying those other aspects of one's life that is affecting one's ability to receive or become open to the healing that is present for everyone. Reiki and Shamanism hold in common the belief that Energy is an expression of the Universal Life Force or Source. Including the emphasis on harmony and balance of the Native American teachings and combining them with the Celtic understanding of the spiraling nature of energy throughout the human body and all of nature itself, creates mystical and healing possibilities that are powerful in a synergistic explosion of healing for myself and for the world in which I live. I am in awe of and I am grateful for the gifts that I have been given throughout this journey to this understanding.

I understand Reiki to be both supported by and supportive of Shamanism. Energy is energy and healing is healing after all, but there are subtle (and sometimes not so subtle) differences. In both cases, there is the irrefutable belief that the energy does not come from the practitioner themselves but through the practitioner when they are thoroughly grounded, centered, and emptied of all ego.

That also means that both traditions rely on the willingness of the Shaman or Reiki practitioner to do the extremely challenging work of getting to that place. There is a shared understanding of healing as that which brings wholeness though not necessarily a cure. Both Reiki practitioners and Shamans are 'works in progress'. They can be sick, face challenges, and struggle with all manner of life circumstances. What matters is their ability to be open to wholeness and healing for themselves, so they can bring wholeness and healing to others. All healing considers the highest good of the person requesting healing as well as for the community and the world.

Shamanism is based in a commitment to the earth, to Mother Earth and all that live and reside inside and outside of her plenteous essence. Reiki sends healing to the earth and advocates for the healing of the entire world. Both traditions believe in distance healing and healing beyond the limits of linear time.

My spiritual practices have changed greatly in my healing journey. When I want to enter a Shamanic journey, I begin by performing a self-Reiki treatment to illuminate whatever needs special attention. I balance and clear my chakras in the order prescribed in Celtic practice, and open my whole being as preparation to make a journey. There is something quite magical in a practice that begins with soothing music that usually accompanies Reiki and Chakra work, and then slowly, in pace with the breath, moves into the more ecstatic beat of the drum which draws the open heart and soul deep into the journey itself. This three-fold energy meditation is now my primary spiritual practice as I move toward the state of harmony and balance much like that which propels Native Americans to experience transcendence. I try to live in gratitude and humility and spend regular time outdoors and seek guidance from my Power Animal (Turtle) and Spirit Guides (Maralda and Ciorcal, in particular). I am open to what comes into my life although I do not always like it. I claim my illness for what it is—an illness.

That which is most significant is our calling to be whole amid physical, mental, or spiritual challenges. If we are fully open to the pathways that await us on our multi-layered journey, we will experience many travels in the Source of Energy and Love. We expand our idea of health and know that a 'cure' may or may not be in our highest good. But wholeness always is. We are Love itself and Love is never lacking or broken. Our journeys are interwoven in our spiritual and emotional and physical pathways. We step into the ground of healing, hear both the call to healing and our response to it; and turn to receive, even bask in the Light of all Light, Energy of all Energy and Love of all Love.

17

The Web of Age: Elder, Crone, Healer

What is there to say about being old? If I make the mistake of saying "I am old" to most people, they will invariably inform me that I am not old. But I am. In the world of 'starting over', I am terribly, terribly old. I struggle daily with the thought of my time running out before I have found everything for which I am looking. People, particularly older than I, try to convince me that I don't even know the nature of being 'old'. And, I want to scream at most of them (and at a rare few I do), "But look what you have to show for all your years—the memories, the financial security you enjoy now, the lasting relationships that have brought you extraordinary joy." The longest relationship I ever had was with the abusive woman from whom I could not escape and that was for 11 years (minus the 9 months I managed to stay away from her). I once figured out that for me to enjoy a relationship as long as many of my friends, I would have to live well into my 90's. And, while I could, it's not something most of us count on. And, indeed, that would require me to begin a relationship tomorrow.

I have few stories to tell of trips to far off places or of new homes or exciting jobs. I have plenty of stories to tell of crying myself to sleep night after night, of driving my car down roads I did not know, screaming at whomever was out there listening, that I was miserable and did not know where to turn. I have plenty of stories of looking at the moon and stars and wishing only for someone to share those with me. This is a downward spiral which seems, at times, as if there is no limit. I want to be okay with my current situation, but to do so, would require a super-human effort, which I currently do not have.

So, I look for what else is out there—what other identity there is for me to claim. And I am at once drawn to embrace the knowledge that I am a crone, an elder. After 60+ years of undiagnosed mental illness, thousands of hours engaged in spiritual study and healing activities, I believe that I have earned the right to consider myself an elder—a crone—if you will, in this community of spiritual healers, wounded healers, and those who live within the unending mystical web of mental illness and sacred transformation. My transformation process is 'old as the hills' and as profound as any other. And so, I claim the title Crone though others may tell me that I am not old enough to be such, I know that I am in all the ways that matter, and I am moving ever more gracefully into that role in my heart and my community.

This does not mean that my life and the memories that I do and do not hold, somehow, suddenly become easy. Nothing is further from the truth. But this knowledge of an identity, a purpose, a reason to be—if you will—makes the pain a little easier to bear. I still struggle with the idea of walking into a room alone. Because I am single, the role of 'third wheel' or 'fifth wheel' (or even 'eleventh wheel') does not appeal to me at all—terrorizes me is the better word, but I no longer feel that I have to fake my comfort. And, sometimes, when I really want to, I just say "no, thank you".

I am a survivor and a wounded healer. With that comes responsibility for my well-being and compassion to myself and to others. I am responsible for my own wholeness, that wholeness that wells up from inside and brings me back up the spiral—even kicking and screaming—and places me where I need to be. Spoiler alert—I still whine at times, I still regret things I have done, and I still mourn the loss of things—of memories and a sense of material security that I may never have, but when I embraced my roles as Crone, as Shaman, as Wounded Healer, I found coherence in my greater life. And, I am grateful, and open to what the future holds. Still sad, at times, but peaceful and contented at least part of the time—something I never had before. And, I am grateful that this status as 'crone' brings with it great gifts, abilities, lessons learned and the willingness to give my all to promote my own healing and the healing of others and the world. I promised myself authenticity, even though my friends may try their best to convince me that I am far too young to be a Crone, an Elder, a 'senior survivor', I welcome this stage in my life, not as a giving up to age and sorrow, but as an affirmation of all that has been, all that is, and all that will come to be.

It sometimes still surprises me that people do not hesitate to tell me that they know better than I do what is best for me. Unless I am in an active stage of mania (which I have not been in for several years now) or getting ready to hurt myself or others, no one knows better than I do what is in the interest of my highest good. And that is what makes me an elder. I do not give advice unless asked (something that takes years to learn) I can only bring the age-old listening heart of the Universe to bear on my interactions. I do not always succeed, but I always try to relax into this new role of mine and let it provide me with intention and purpose. It always amazes me when someone thanks me for helping them. Ninety percent of the time I have done nothing but hold open a holy space for sacred listening.

I cannot help but wonder at times how different my life would have been if someone had known how and desired to listen and hear and accept the anguished words of a beautiful young girl who was drowning in her own sorrow and despair. I learned through my own painful and meandering journeys that the yearning to be heard is intrinsic to who we are. That learning filled me with a life-long desire to be someone who could listen. In 1960, Taylor Caldwell wrote *The Listener*, I was 8-years-old. I found myself drawn to the book by the time I was 11 or 12. As I began to read and re-read this story, my heart ached for someone to listen. Although it was not one of her most famous books, it certainly touched the divinity in that small child. And it gave me hope that someday I would meet such a listener. I have had people play that role throughout my life but never to the extent for which I wished (perhaps I was asking something that no human can give).

This yearning gave me the courage and desire to become such a person. I work to quiet my own voices and give way to the only voice that matters now—the one in front of me. This wisdom is the meaning of the appellation 'Crone' and I am humbled to wear it regardless of others' expectations.

In my role as Elder and Crone, I am living out my calling to be a wounded healer. I am allowing that woundedness to surface, to matter, and to change the way I regard my own suffering. I am able during that radical transformation to feel my link to the Sacred, the Universal Source of Love. More importantly, I find myself ready to be a conduit of that love, to become the connection between Energy, Source, and those who have a need to experience that connection. This is not to say that I never doubt my ability to be such a person 100% of the time. Perhaps, I will achieve that someday, but right now, I am simply on my way.

I have learned to begin to embrace the scars that I carry as a sign of my surviving what many people do not. I have been graced and gifted, and it is time for me to return that giftedness to those who need what I have learned and to the earth.

18

And So It Is: Blessed Be

It is hard to accept times of darkness into our lives, our hearts. But they come, nevertheless. I felt at many times in my life completely out of control and lost for a way to understand what was happening to me. My long connection to Spirit whispered to me over the years that if I was able to fully accept the darkness, the Light would shine through it. I wanted to believe that if I could welcome the darkness inside and hold it in a warm embrace it would transform my heart. I fought the darkness, I will admit, but mostly, I just did not want to succumb to it as I feared it might pull me down into its chaos forever.

I do not think that I was or am alone. The fear of darkness, and of seemingly uncontrollable thoughts racing through my already exhausted fragile brain caused me to live my life for the first six decades as almost always afraid of 'going off the deep end'. I didn't always know what that might look like. I knew it might involve giving up and floating into full-blown psychosis, hospitalization (and I had seen too many clients—both parents and children flail about in an institutional setting to accept that) or, in the worst case, suicide. Now fortunately for me, early in my life, I was terrified of dying, or at least terrified of not succeeding only to leave myself in a permanently injured body in which I would then have to live out the rest of my life. It was not always bravery that kept me alive, it was sometimes just unadulterated fear. Whatever kept me alive, I'm glad that it did. As I grew older, this fear was less intense and the call of suicide somehow stronger, particularly in my last profound episode.

However, when I truly 'reached the end of my rope', I began to know that I had some choices to make. More than anything, I wanted to know if I could make some sense, find any coherence, come to any understanding why my life was just so incredibly unmanageable. I wanted to know how the pieces fit and how to find a way to leave something to the world—not because I planned to die—but because I knew I would someday, and I wanted my life to matter. In that search, I learned many important things (and the search is far from over). I learned, first and foremost, that I do matter, perhaps not in ways that I had envisioned myself 'mattering', but in ways that I could only begin to imagine.

Fortunately, because I was no longer working, I had the luxury of devoting time to my healing and finding my way back into the world. I began to know that in the journey to embrace my vulnerabilities there was the potential for love and wholeness. I also knew that my return to my place in this world as a healer was inevitable—my call had not disappeared because of my illness and I was given the opportunity to pour my woundedness into my yearning to be whole and to accompany others in their yearning to be whole. And this became the most important thing for me to do in that moment.

The aftermath of my wild and tangled life still needed addressing and I was doing that—not with joy or even relief but because I had to.

I'd like to claim that I never wanted to give up again. That would be far more than just false, it would be downright dishonest. One of the many things that I have learned and come to embrace is that there are worse things than rejection and loneliness and being untrue to your own story is one of them. And so, in this somewhat quiet period I had some hard things to do. I knew that I had to allow my heart to heal, but to keep that longing for hope, for change, for purpose alive during the healing. I did not just need healing, I needed to use my healing for good.

More than anything, I wanted to change and yet embrace all that I was, all that I had lived through, and all that was left to do. I wanted to know what it looked like to be the me I was now and had always been—a wounded healer—after coming to terms with my diagnosis, learning (in tiny steps) how to live a full life despite the vulnerabilities, the need for a special kind of self-care, reliance on medication (in my case) to deal with the worst of the symptoms, and the need to continue in my spiritual evolution that had both saved me and moved me toward the chaotic manifestations of my mis-firing mind. All my life, at least all of it that I could remember, was consumed by this quest. I realized in my actual homelessness in a body that had seemingly betrayed me, that I needed, more than anything to find a way home. The symptoms that accompanied this 'betrayal' were the twists and turns on the road-map that led me to the place I most needed to be in life, in Spirit, in self and in the world.

I know that in this search for meaning, for hope, for future, I have indeed come 'home'—home to who I always was but with a depth of understanding that enables me to continue to burrow deep into my own wounding and discover and enlarge the light that illuminates my soul. It has both surprised and excited me. I am who I have always been even though I did not have a consciousness of just who that was. I no longer live according to others' expectations or within the confines of beliefs that I have placed on myself. Every day I experience new ways of being whole.

But there is more. I have often tried to convince myself that growth is always in a forward movement and that stepping backwards is somehow a negative thing. Not so. Sometimes after a great spiritual 'growth spurt' I continue to find it necessary to be quiet, gently waiting for what is next; even moving backwards a bit while I 'catch up' spiritually with what I have learned. I found that it is important for me to be able to experience and deepen spiritual growth and not just 'aha' moments separated from life-lived context. This requires me to be willing to be flexible, gently moving forward; yet, having no fear for the backward steps when necessary. In this gentle dance of forwards, backwards, and sideways, I move in Spirit and settle in stillness.

From my Spirit Guide, Maralda, "What is there except hope? You can surround yourself in a haze of despair, anxiety, and confusion or you can blow away that very fog with a mighty puff of breath that says, 'no, I want to breathe in all that Spirit has to give me.' It matters not your physical condition, financial fears, or pain of loneliness. Spirit longs to give you hope. You confuse hope with instant miracle. Hope simply means that you are willing to wait, that you are ready to hear, and that you will find the courage to step into whatever Light is in front of you. This means loving yourself enough to be there when Spirit reveals your next step. Look up. Fondly, Maralda."[82]

When I sat down to begin this closing section, I expected to feel relief or some sense of completion. Instead, I found myself slammed with an overwhelming sense of fatigue. Even with my new understanding and an increased sense of coherence in my life I find that in order to celebrate all of that and all that still lies ahead—which I am looking forward to—it is important for me to acknowledge that my life has been hard. 60 plus years of depression and anxiety, fear, and abuse takes its toll. I find myself wondering sometimes what my life would have looked like had I received a diagnosis at 25 or even 30.

I'd like to be able to tell you that I no longer regret the time I spent in the midst of Bipolar mania or depression when I could have been making better decisions or growing in my understanding of spirituality instead of merely studying it—hoping for some enlightenment to appear on the horizon fulfilling my deepest yearning to understand all I longed to understand. There are times, yes even many times, when I want back all the hours I spent begging 'God' for answers. Suddenly, seemingly out of nowhere, I want to flail my arms and say, "no, no, no—I don't want to be talking about mental illness, about myself and about all it has meant in my life and in the lives of those around me." And, finally, when the raging pain has passed, I come again to the sweet spot of understanding we reach when we realize that we go where we go by different paths. And I don't have to like mine; I was never required to like it.

What I know now, though, is that in order for my life, in its entirety, to have the meaning, the healing, and, yes, the coherence I have longed for, I have to embrace the pain, the torture even, the regret, resentment, and resistance and love myself enough to bring all those parts of my fairly long experience with mental illness AND spirituality into the wholeness I have already found and the greater wholeness that awaits. It is no surprise I am tired. To try to convince you otherwise would be dishonest; and, it would seem downright ridiculous at this point in this brutally honest book, to do anything except continue to be honest. So, I am tired. I am also hopeful in ways I have never been before, and both things are true at once. It is not unusual, and, in fact, is quite predictable that spiraling upward and downward can and do occur at the same time. It is the nature of mental illness and spirituality, both influenced by the simple nature of life. In my crazy swirling search for center and understanding I was thrown from spiral to spiral much as if two tornados occupied the same pasture simultaneously.

Even in my toughest times, I never gave up trying to understand what was going on in my life, my brain, and my heart. Because of all the conflicting messages that I received from the world, from my spiritual captivity to ways that I believed I should believe, and the swirling, whirling of my fragile mind I experienced an inability to hear, much less listen to the messages that I was receiving from my body and heart in the undercurrent of life. Long before I began such a process, I had a lengthy list—a long ugly list—of all the things I thought I was, and those characteristics were not pretty. I was constantly amazed that I could carry out what I accomplished in my life when I believed that this long (ugly) list of attributes truly described who I was. It never occurred to me, even when I desperately wanted it to be so, that this long disagreeable list of negative attributes was not the entirety of who I was. In fact, it was not who I was at all. I had challenges that I had faced and would need to face again, but I knew I was more than all that.

I am, in fact, who I have always been—a woman of integrity, of capabilities (some quite significant), of kindness, and of passion and compassion. Even in my darkest times I searched for ways to be a friend to the friendless and give compassion to those who needed it. My mental illness did not render me incapable of knowing right from wrong although it did at times make it less likely I would make the best decision for myself. I was fortunate that neither my impulsivity nor my self-hatred altered my consciousness of reality; but both made it much more difficult to ignore the quiet whispers of "this is not good for you". This knowing and inability to act is the sort of paradox that exists with mental illness and it is my constant reality. It is also my constant source of hope.

Spiritually I wanted to belong to something much greater than I had experienced. I wanted my life to touch others in ways that I had been unable to access. I knew that I was called to be a healer, but I didn't yet know how to find the way to healing for myself. Instinctively, I understood that self-healing, and more importantly, self-love were pre-requisites for all I wanted to be in my soul. My mental illness clouded my thinking and sometimes made it impossible for me to think at all. Anxiety, panic attacks, PTSD, and crippling depression kept me imprisoned in agonizing self-doubt and paralyzing fear. And, yet, in the crevices of my heart, was a tiny little spark of hope that someday, if not that day, something or someone would intervene. I had no idea how painful and terrifying that intervention would turn out to be, but when it came, and when I surfaced from its depths, I knew this life-exploding event would change me forever.

First came a change in my approach and a different kind of seeking to understand. I willed myself to stop begging the Universe to grant me some small measure of comprehension and began to look for that insight on my own terms. But they were not easy terms. I learned that I could not ignore the need for honest self-evaluation and an accounting of the circumstances I needed to confront. This takes great courage—this digging deep and facing the truth—my truth and not what someone else believes my truth to be. When people or circumstances bring me pain rather than strength and prevent me from learning all there is to learn about myself, I must make changes. People, even well-meaning people, who would seek to limit my moving into my fullest potential, if they cannot accept and embrace my changes, I may be required to leave them behind. When I know what I know at a deeper, more profound level, I have a new responsibility to choose more wisely and to work for my own higher good and the higher good of others.

There were many circumstances that were bringing pain into my life. One was the physical symptoms of the disease itself. As much as I did not want to undertake a medication regimen, I knew that, after my collapse, the gig was up. There was no more pretending; I simply did not have it in me. And while I am more than willing to say, and say loudly, that medication is not a panacea for mental illness; and that, in fact, the use of it brings great sacrifice, the paradox is that utilizing medication to get my feet back on the ground is exactly what I needed to do. I also needed to develop many alternative ways to help me deal with the symptoms that medication did not relieve as well as the side effects of the medication itself. Though met with mixed feelings by many, I have chosen to live out the paradox of relying on the use of medication for dealing with the mis-firing in my brain and the worst of the symptoms that made it impossible for me to 'get on with it' while living into the sacred transformation that accompanies the growth of healing.

Because of the never-ending struggle with mental illness, I allowed my vulnerabilities to determine who I could be and what I could do. This limitation of all that I have affected me both spiritually and mentally. Internalizing stigma and shame, I believed that I was 'not enough' for the Sacred Source to love and embrace. Nor did I allow myself to accept love and care for me from others until, of course, I had no choice. I cared deeply for others, spent all my working years in places where my responsibilities required me to feel compassion for others; and yet, found myself incapable of genuinely believing that I was worthy of that same love and compassion from others or from myself.

I was also, consciously, or unconsciously, allowing the expectations of others and my own expectations of myself to keep me from coming into my own power. It took a giant breaking down of the walls that I had erected to protect those expectations both as a spiritual person and as a person who integrated profound depression, anxiety, and panic into my daily life. I had come to expect to be depressed just as I had come to expect myself to remain uncomfortable with the incongruency of my inner and outer spiritual life. I was living my life in the center of the vortex of the spiral although instead of experiencing an infusion of energy, I was sucked dry on every level. The curves of the spiral tore at me because I still believed I could 'do it all'. On both a spiritual level and a psychic level I was, oh, so wrong.

I know now that I had, and in many ways continue to have a 'sacred illness'. Deena Metzger, poet, novelist, essayist, storyteller, teacher, healer and medicine woman who has taught and counseled for over fifty years, explains, "A sacred illness is one that educates us and alters us from the inside out, provides experiences and therefore knowledge that we could not possibly achieve in any other way, and aligns us with a life path that is, ultimately, of benefit to ourselves and those around us."[83]

To come to believe that mental illness is, indeed, a 'sacred illness' enabled me to grant myself the freedom to explore and reclaim my initial vocation of 'wounded healer'. My first 'wounding' came as a young child and my ability to be of service to others and to communities grew throughout my life. What I did not have was a true understanding of healing for myself. I labored for years in the belief that if I could be healed, I would be cured. I did not grasp the difference between the two. And based on my early beliefs and my own innate perfectionism, I felt as though if I were not cured from my mental illness (even though I did not know its name) that I could not be healed. My sacred illness remained patient with me until it no longer could. My heart blew wide apart from the weight of all that I had carried so that room opened for all that I would come to know. A broken heart is an open heart. My heart had been broken many, many times, and so there were many cracks and places where light could seep in and begin the 'healing' process. In that fiery explosion now several years ago, many of those thoughts and beliefs about myself and the world were literally blown sky-high—so high, fortunately—that my knowledge of who I thought myself to be and what I thought the world to be were shredded and sent into the Universe for transformation.

I do not underestimate the severity of my sacred illness, nor the dangerous nature of it. If I did not understand this, I do not know that I could have listened to my heartbeat of courage and yearning for enlightenment. Although I had been trying to hear for decades, it took this shattering of all that I believed myself to be so that I could be present to the vibration of change and healing, longing to saturate my now empty soul. I am not alone in this experience, of course. There are millions of stories to tell and to hear, and I hope that this book provides encouragement for others to tell their stories both of struggle and of healing as well.

I do not always gracefully accept that my healing is ongoing— that I will continue to contend with issues and conditions that I believed I had fully explored and placed in a box secured tightly with tape and placed in the closet of the past. However, in a book I have come to treasure, *All Sickness is Homesickness*, Dianne Connelly proposes a greater understanding. "The wise woman", she says, "who allies herself with the tides of the universe also comes to the understanding that our healing is cyclic as well. A deep-rooted issue does not go away with one turn of the Wheel. The wise woman has learned that the path of growth is spiraled. With each turn, we ascend upward. We may have to face the same painful lessons over and over again, but they change because our position on the spiral has changed. We look at it from a different perspective, and in so doing, reveal a deeper layer of the shadow and a higher level of the self."[84]

And, so what we learn is that our own spiritual work does not end with some magical transformation from which we emerge wholly immersed in our own healing and in the healing of others. I labored some with coming to an understanding of what healing might look like for me. I had answered a naïve call to become a healer at 18 or 19. I did not know exactly what that meant; and, of course, over the course of my life it has meant many different things. As a creative person, as many people with mental illness are, I instinctively knew, that whatever direction my life might take that somehow the ability to create would intertwine. People do not often link the ideas of healing and creativity in our thoughts about Spirit. Nevertheless, the linkage is not only logical, it is magical. When healing is taking place, it is through the creativity of my body to make itself new. My body re-creates itself at amazing rates; and, yet I seldom stop to appreciate the constant regeneration of my cells, my energies, and my very being. This seems to be true whether I am in a period of health or a period of illness. And yet, I may be moving towards greater and fuller health or toward a peaceful, graceful transition into another state of being. Creativity requires the very same sense of surrender to Spirit. I can try or study, but the truth is that I am creative only when I enter the place where Spirit is All That Is, and I am thrown headlong into the eruption of creativity that produces an experience identical to the re-creation of our bodies. I cannot control either; I am gifted by both.

Creativity is one expression of living from our deeper selves. And that is the gift that got me through the ups and downs, and ins and outs of the weave of mental illness within spiritual journey and spiritual journey within mental illness. Sandra Ingerman, speaking of those who have answered the call to become Shamans, says: "Part of doing your personal work is learning how to live from your heart and be guided through life by your heart and your strong eye—where you have access to your intuition. You cannot see through the challenges which life contains. And you cannot power through with the strength of only your body and mind. The strength of your spirit will carry you through."[85]

Visionary Deena Metzger notes, "It is not unusual for illness to lead to vision, but we err in not fully understanding its implications. We are conversant with the idea of the wounded healer, but we do not fully recognize that the making of a healer may well be the positive function of illness, a call, on behalf of the world, to every person who suffers. Illness is the breakdown that requires re-organization. Without that breakdown, the re-visioning and re-organization may not occur… Illness is not the enemy; it is the messenger."[86]

So, I am a vastly different woman from the one who began this journey as a young, misunderstood, and mistreated girl. I lived through my adolescence with the rage against myself and 'God' continuing to grow until one day, I collapsed into the oblivion of unrelenting pain. The depression and anxiety would stay with me throughout my young adult years even as I searched unsuccessfully for ways to understand what I was supposed to understand. In my 30's PTSD, Panic, Addictions, and Self-Harm were added to my ever-growing list of things it seemed

I could not control. My spirituality seemed out of control as well, leading me first one way and then the next. I was lost in every way. Within the next 10 years or so, thoughts that seemed heretical at the time, slowly began to surface contributing to my guilt and fear of rejection and of the pain that seemed certainly on the horizon. As life continued to unfold, I began to change, in many ways, not always knowing the difference between the helpful and unhelpful.

And, within years of turning 60, my life crashed into the wall that had lurked before me in shadowy mists my entire life. The collision of my mental, physical, and spiritual catastrophic journeys dropped me into a place of no return. I could not relive the meandering ways that had brought me to this place. Once I managed to circumnavigate the wall itself, I could only go forward or give up altogether. I am grateful that I did not stop searching, striving, and looking for the good in my life—the beautiful—and the brave.

At the edge of a forest wilderness I stand.

Seeking a path—finding there is none.

Revealing the need to forge a way for myself.

Trees, both friendly and terrifying

welcome me to this longing for peace—

this spiraling high through the branches,

lifting my spirit high to Moon, Stars, and Sun—

this resting in the roots centering my heart

deep, deep, deep into Mother Earth.

Standing, waiting, unsure of what to do.

The gentle whisper of the wind in the trees

and the scurry of animals in the underbrush

remind me to listen to the gentle calling of Spirit,

the tender yearnings of my heart,

and to know that I carry the

Source of Light inside.

It will show the way.

I need only take those first few steps in courage

and the rest will come—one step at a time.

I stand bravely and place foot in front of foot

in trust that my Inner Light will not fail.

C. Chambers, August 2018

BIBLIOGRAPHY

Buddhism and Taoism

Chödrön, Pema. *When Things Fall Apart: Heart Advice for Difficult Times.* Boulder, CO: Shambhala Publications, 1997.

Beck, Charlotte Joko. *Nothing Special: Living Zen.* New York, NY: Harper One, 1991.cf

Gattuso, Joan. *The Lotus Still Blooms: Sacred Buddhist Teachings for the Western Mind.* New York, NY: Jeremy P. Tarcher/Penguin, 2008.

Gyatso, Geshe Kelsang. *Modern Buddhism: The Path of Compassion and Wisdom.* Tharpa Publishers, March 31, 2015. Kindle.

Johanson, Greg and Ron Kurtz. *Grace Unfolding: Psychotherapy in the Spirit of the Tao-te ching.* New York, NY: Bell Tower, 1991.

Trungpa, Chögyam. *The Path Is The Goal.* Boston and London: Shambhala, 2010.

Van Der Hoeven, Joanna. *Zen for Druids: A Further Guide to Integration, Compassion and Harmony with Nature.* Alresfoord, Hants, UK: John Hunt Publishing, Moon Books, 2016.

Celtic Tradition

Beth, Tudor. *The Celtic Hedge-Witch.* Amazon Digital Services, 2018. Kindle.

Bonwick, James. *Irish Druids.* Amazon Digital Services, 2013.

Conway, D.J. *By Oak, Ash, & Thorn: Modern Celtic Shamanism.* Woodbury, MN: Llewellyn Publications, 1995.

Freeman, Mara. *Kindling the Celtic Spirit.* San Francisco, CA: Harper, 2001.

Hidalgo, Sharlyn. *The Healing Power of Trees*. Amazon Digital Services, 2010. Kindle.

James, Catrin. *Celtic Faery Shamanism*. Freshfields Chieveley Berks: Capall Bann Pub., 1998.

MacEOwen, Frank. *The Celtic Way of Seeing: Meditations on the Irish Spirit Wheel*. Novato, CA: New World Library, 2007.

MacEOwen, Frank. *The Mist-Filled Path: Celtic Wisdom for Exiles, Wanderers, and Seekers*. Novato, CA: New World Library, 2002

McIntosh, Kenneth. *Water from an Ancient Well: Celtic Spirituality for Modern Life*. Anamchara Books, 2011.

Matthews, Caitlín. *Singing the Soul Back Home: Shamanic Wisdom for Every Day*. Boston: Connections Publishing, 1995, 2002.

O'Donohue, John. *Anam Cara: A Book of Celtic Wisdom*. New York, NY: Harper Perennial, 1997.

O'Donohue, John. *Eternal Echoes: Celtic Reflections on Our Yearning to Belong*. New York, NY: Harper Collins, 1999.

O'Donohue, John. *To Bless the Space Between Us*. New York, NY: Doubleday, 2008.

Sentier, Elen. *The Awen Alone: Walking the Path of the Solitary Druid*. Amazon Digital Services, 2014. Kindle.

Sentier, Elen. *The Celtic Chakras*. Winchester, UK: Moon Books, 2013.

Sentier, Elen. *The Druid Shaman: Exploring the Celtic Otherworld*. Amazon Digital Services, 2014. Kindle.

Sentier, Elen. *Merlin: Once and Future Wizard*. Amazon Digital Services, 2014.

Sentier, Elen. *Trees of the Goddess: A New Way of Working With the Ogham*. Amazon Digital Services, 2013. Kindle.

Sigillito, Gina, Sile Deady, and Patricia Kin. *The Wisdom of the Celts*. New York, NY: Citadel Press, 2004.

Van Der Hoeven, Joanna. *The Awen Alone: Walking the Path of the Solitary Druid*. Alresford, Hants, UK: Moon Books, 2014.

Van Gelder, Dora. *The Real World of Fairies*. Wheaton, IL: Quest Books. 1977,1999.

Lyn Webster Wilde. *Becoming the Enchanter: A Journey to the Heart of the Celtic Mysteries.* NY: Jeremy P. Tarcher/Penguin, 2002.

Chakras

Judith, Anodea. *Chakra Balancing: Workbook.* Boulder, CO: Sounds True, 2003. With accompanying compact disc.

Judith, Anodea. *Eastern Body Western Mind: Psychology and The Chakra System as a Path to the Self.* Berkeley, CA: Celestial Arts, 2004.

Elise, Kerry. *Chakra Mastery for Balancing and Healing.* Amazon Digital Services, 2014. Kindle.

Simpson, Liz. *The Book of Chakra Healing.* New York, NY: Sterling Ethos, 2013.

Wauters, Ambika. *Chakras and their Archetypes: Uniting Energy Awareness and Spiritual Growth.* Freedom, CA: The Crossing Press, 1997.

White, Ruth. *Working with Your Chakras: A Physical, Emotional & Spiritual Approach.* York Beach, ME: Samuel Weiser Inc, 1993.

Christian Mystics

Chittister, Joan. *Beyond the Dark and the Daylight: Embracing the Contradictions of Life.* NY: Random House, 2014. Kindle.

Chittister, Joan D. *Scarred by Struggle, Transformed by Hope.* Grand Rapids, MI: Will B. Eerdmans Publishing Company, 2003.

Fox, Matthew. *Christian Mystics.* Novato, CA. New World Library, 2011.

Frenette, David and Father Thomas Keating. *The Path of Centering Prayer: Deepening Your Experience of God.* Amazon Digital Services, 2012.

Jones, Alan. *Soul Making: The Desert Way of Spirituality.* New York: Harper and Row, 1985.

May, Gerald G. *The Dark Night of the Soul: A Psychiatrist Explores the Connection Between Darkness and Spiritual Growth.* San Francisco: Harper, 2005.

Palmer, Parker. *A Hidden Wholeness: The Journey Toward an Undivided Life.* San Francisco: Josey-Bass, 2004.

Palmer, Parker. *Let Your Life Speak. Listening to the Voice of Vocation.* San Francisco: Wiley and Smith, 2000.

Teasdale, Wayne. *The Mystic Heart.* New World Library, 2001.

Energy Healing

Dale, Cyndi. *Subtle Energy Techniques.* Woodbury, MN: Llewellyn Publications, 2017.

White, Ruth. *Energy Healing for Beginners.* New York: Jeremy P. Tarcher/Putnam, 2002.

White, Ruth. *Working with Your Soul.* London: Platkus, 2007.

Mental Illness and Spirituality

Curtis, Theresa. Broken Open: Transformation through Trauma". Sage Woman, Issue 92., 19.

Green-McCreight, Kathryn. *Darkness Is My Only Companion: A Christian Response to Mental Illness.* Grand Rapids, MI: Brazos Press, 2006.

Holstein, Alice A. *A Tough Grace: Mental Illness as a Spiritual Path.* Essex UK: Chipmunk Publishing, 2011.

May, Gerald. *Simply Sane: The Spirituality of Mental Health.* New York, NY: The Crosswood Publishing Company, 1977.

Sorrell, Stephanie. *Depression as a Spiritual Journey.* Winchester, UK: O-Books, 2009.

General

Brach, Tara. *Radical Acceptance.* New York: Bantam, 2004. Kindle.

Campbell, Joseph. *Myths to Live By.* Amazon Digital Services, 2011. Kindle.

Campbell, Joseph with Bill Moyers. The Power of Myth. New York: Anchor Books. 1991.

Connelly, Dianne M., *All Sickness is Home Sickness: An Inspiring Book about Illness, Healing, and Living.* Unknown Publisher, 1993.

Keen, Sam and Ann Valley-Fox. *Your Mythic Journey: Finding Meaning in Your Life through Writing and Storytelling.* New York, NY: Jeremy P. Tarcher/Penguin, 1973,1990.

Lionberger, John. *Renewal in the Wilderness: A Spiritual Guide to Connecting with God in the Natural World.* Woodstock. VT: Sunlight Paths Publishing, 2007.

Millman, Dan. *Everyday Enlightenment: The Twelve Gateways to Personal Growth.* New York: Warner Books, 1998.

Millman, Dan. *Wisdom of the Peaceful Warrior.* Peaceful Warrior ePublishing, 2010. Kindle.

Pendegergast, John. "In Touch with Your Inner Knowing," *Mind, Body Spirit,* Winter 2017, Issue 52.

Roberts, Llyn. *The Good Remembering A Message for Our Times.* Winchester, U.K.: O Books, 2007.

Rooks. Diane. *Spinning Gold out of Straw: How Stories Heal.* St. Augustine Press: Salt Run Press, 2001.

Giesemann, Suzanne. *Droplets of God: The Life and Philosophy of Mavis Pattilla.* USA, One Mind Books, 2019.

Taylor, Barbara Brown. *Leaving Church: A Memoir of Faith.* Harper-Collins E-book, 2009.Kindle.

Meditation and Mindfulness

Kabat-Zinn, Jon. *Full Catastrophe Living: Using the Wisdom of Your Body and Your Body and Mind to Face Stress Pain and Illness.* New York, NY: Delta, 1990.

Kabat-Zinn, Jon. *Wherever You Go There You Are.* New York, NY: Hyperion, 1994.

Thich Nhat Hanh. *The Bells of Mindfulness.* Penguin Random House Publisher Services, 2013. Kindle.

Mental Illness

McMurrich Roberts, Stephanie, Louisa Grandin Sylvia, and Noreen A. Reilly-Harrington. *The Bipolar II Disorder Workbook: Managing Recurring Depression, Hypomania, and Anxiety.* New Harbinger Publications; Workbook edition, 2014.

Duke, Patty and Gloria Hochman. *A Brilliant Madness: Living with Depressive Illness. New York:* Bantam, 2010. Kindle.

Fisher, Carrie. *Wishful Drinking.* New York. Simon and Schuster Paperbooks, 2009.

Phillips, Jim. *Why Am I Still Depressed?* New York: McGraw-Hill Education, 2006.

Simon, Tami, ed. *Darkness Before Dawn: Redefining the Journey through Depression.* Boulder Colorado: Sounds True, 2015.

Simpkins, C. Alexander and Annellen M. Simpkins. *The Tao of Bipolar: Using Meditation and Mindfulness to Find Balance and Peace.* New Harbinger Publications, 2013.

Native American

Benner, Mara. "Native American Healing". https://fourdirectionswellness.com/native-american-healing/.

Ewing, Jim Pathfinder. "Using the Medicine Wheel to Bring Balance to the Earth". https://www.manataka.org/page694.html.

Garrett, J.T. and Michael Garrett. *Medicine of the Cherokee: The Way of Right Relationship.* Rochester, VT: Bear & Company, 1996.

Garrett, J.T. and Michael Tlanusta Garrett. *The Cherokee Full Circle: A Practical Guide to Ceremonies and Traditions.* Rochester, VT: Bear & Company, 2002.

Garrett, Michael T. *Walking on the Wind: Cherokee Teaching for Harmony and Balance.* Sante Fe, NM: Bear & Company, 1998.

Praying Wolf, Jewel. "Healing Totem". https://www.nlm.nih.gov/nativevoices/exhibition/healing-totem/index.html.

Meadows, Kenneth. *Earth Medicine: Revealing Hidden Teachings of the Native American Medicine Wheel.* Shaftsbury, Dorset, UK: Element, 1989, 1996.

Meadows, Kenneth. *The Medicine Way: How to Live the Teachings of the Native Medicine Wheel—A Shamanic Path to Self-Mastery.* Shaftsbury, Dorset, UK: Element, 1990.

Newburn, Kent, ed. *The Wisdom of the Native Americans.* Novato, CA: New World Library, 1999.

Sams, Jamie. *Dancing the Dream: the Seven Sacred Paths of Human Transformation.* New York, NY: Harper Collins, 1998.

Sams, Jamie. *The 13 Original Clan Mothers: Your Sacred Path to Discovering the Gifts, Talents & Abilities of the Feminine Through the Ancient Teachings of the Sisterhood.* New York, NY: Harper One, 1994.

"Traditional Native American Healing Methods". https://sites. google.com/site/nativeamericanshealingmethods/home/ traditional-native-american-healing-methods.

Reiki

Ellis, Richard. *Reiki and the Seven Chakras: Your Essential Guide.* London: Vermilion, 2002.

Green, Janet. *The Reiki Healing Handbook.* New York, NY: Chartwell Press, 2012,1018.

Honervogt, Tanmaya. *The Power of Reiki: An Ancient Hands-On Healing Technique.* New York, NY: St. Martin's Griffin, 1998.

Keyes, Raven. *The Healing Power of Reiki: A Modern Master's Approach to Emotional, Spiritual & Physical Wellness.* Woodbury, MN: Llewellyn Publications, 2012.

Powers, Lisa. *Reiki: Level I, II and Master Manual.* No publisher. 2016.

Powers, Lisa. *Reiki: Level I, II and Master Class.* Udemy, 2018. ttps://www. udemy.com/reikicourse/learn/v4/overview.

Prasad, Kathleen. *Everything Animal Reiki: A Simple Guide to Meditating with Animals for Healing.* US: Amazon, 2015.

Rand, William Lee. *Reiki for a New Millennium.* Smithfield, MI: Vision Publications, 1998.

Samson, Anne. "Reiki Leads Us on Our True Life Path". *Reiki.* Winter 2017, volume 16, Issue Four, 18.

Shipon, Randolph. *Reiki Psychology.* Amazon Digital Services, 2010.

Shamanic Reiki

Llyn Roberts and Robert Levy. *Shamanic Reiki: Expanded Way of Working with Universal Life Force Energy.* Winchester, UK: O-Books, 2008.

PathFinder Ewing, Jim (Nvnehi Awatisgi). *Dreams of the Reiki Shaman: Expanding Your Healing Power.* Rochester, Vermont: Rochester, Vermont: Findhorm Press, 2011.

PathFinder Ewing, Jim (Nvnehi Awatisgi). *Reiki Shamanism: A Guide to Out-of-Body Healing.* Vermont: Rochester, Vermont: Findhorm Press, 2008.

Rowling, Jena. *Shamanic Reiki Therapy.* Self-Published, 2012.

Shamanism

Baghramian, Arvick. *The Magic of Shamanism.* Guid Publications, 2012.

Charing, Howard G. *The Accidental Shaman: Journeys with Plant Teachers and Other Spirit Allies.* Rochester, VT: Destiny Books, 2017.

Conway, D.J. *By Oak, Ash, & Thorn: Modern Celtic Shamanism.* Woodbury, MN: Llewellyn Worldwide, 2017.

Deatsman, Colleen. *Seeing in the Dark: Claim Your Own Shamanic Power Now and in the Coming Age.* San Francisco, CA: Red Wheel/Weiser, LLC, 2009.

Deatsman, Colleen. *The Hollow Bone A Field Guide to Shamanism.* San Francisco, CA: Weiser Books, 2011.

DeDan, Rose. *Tails of a Healer: Animals, Reiki & Shamanism.* Bloomington, IN: Authorhouse, 2007.

Francis, Paul. *The Shamanic Journey: A Practical Guide to Therapeutic Shamanism.* Amazon Digital Services, 2017.

Gamble, Rebekah, *A Map to Otherworld: The Guide to Meditative Shamanic Journeying.* Blessings Press, 2016.

Ingerman, Sandra. Interview with Christina Pratt "Why Shamanism Now", http://whyshamanismnow.com/2018/10/teens-shamanism-and-hidden-worlds-with-sandra-ingerman/, October 30, 2018.

Ingerman, Sandra. *Shamanic Meditations.* 2010, Sounds True, compact disc.

Ingerman, Sandra. *Soul Retrieval: Mending the Fragmented Self.* New York: Harper One, 1991.

Ingerman, Sandra. *Walking in the Light: the Everyday Empowerment of a Shamanic Life.* Boulder, CO: Sounds True, 2015.

Ingerman, Sandra & Hank Wesselman. *Awakening to the Spirit World: The Shamanic Path of Direct Revelation.* Boulder, CO: Sounds True, 2010.

Ingerman, Sandra and Hank Wesselman. *Awakening to the Spirit World.* 2010, Sounds True, compact disc.

Kahn, Ya'acoy Darling. *Jaguar in the Body Butterfly in the Heart: The Real-Life Initiation of an Everyday Shaman.* Carlsbad, CA: Hay House, 2017.

Kent, J.A. *The Goddess and The Shaman: The Art and Science of Magical Healing.* Woodbury, MN: Llewellyn Publications, 2016.

McAllister, Paul. *My Journeys to the Spirit World.* Amazon Digital Services, 2016.

Mathhews, Caitlín. *Singing the Soul Back Home.* London: Connections Book Publishing, 2002.

Matthews, Caitlín and John. *Walkers Between the Worlds: The Wester Mysteries from Shamanism to Magus.* Rochester, VT, 1985.

Matthews, John. *The Shamanism Bible: The Definitive Guide to Shamanic Thought and Practice.* Buffalo, N.Y.: Firefly Books, 2014.

Moss, Robert. *Dreaming the Soul Back Home: Shamanic Dreaming for Healing and Becoming Whole.* San Francisco, CA: New World Library, 2012.

O'Neil, Ilsya. *Shamanism: A Spiritual Journey.* Self-Published. 2014.

Ramel, Sharon. *Shamanic Initiation for Spiritual Awakening and Liberation, Udemy, 2018.* https://www.udemy.com/munay-ki/learn/v4/overview.

Skaggs, Katherine. *Soul Retrieval Workshop.* Presented on February 16, 2018 at The Villages, Florida.

Smith, Kenneth. *Shamanism for the Age of Science: Awakening the Energy Body.* Rochester, VT: Bear & Company, 2008, 2011.

Somé, Malidoma Patrice. *Ritual: Power, Healing, and Community.* New York, NY: Penguin, 1993.

Villoldo, Alberto. *Mending the Past and Healing the Future with Soul Retrieval.* Carlsbad, CA: Hay House, 2005.

Wanner, Mike, *PTSD and Soul Retrieval: Putting One Back Together.* Amazon Digital Services, 2015.

Williams, Mike. *Follow the Shaman's Call: An Ancient Path for Modern Lives.* Woodbury, MN: Llewellyn Publications, 2017.

Wolfe, Amber. *In the Shadow of the Shaman: Connecting with Self, Nature & Spirit.* St. Paul, MN: Llewellyn Publications, 1996.

Spirit Guides, etc.

Andrews, Ted. *The Intercession of Spirits: Working with Animals, Angels & Ancestors.* Jackson, TN. Dragon hawk Publishing, 2008.

Conway, D J. *Guides Guardians and Angels: Experience Relationships with Your Spiritual Companions.* Woodbury, MN: Llewellyn Publications, 2009.

Curtis, Theresa. "Broken Open: Transformation through Trauma". *Sage Woman*, 92. Fall 2017.

Star, Konstanza Morning. *Medium: a Step-by Step Guide to Communicating with the Spirit World.* Woodbury, MN, 2017.

Van Praagh, James. *Wisdom from Your Spirit Guides: A Handbook to Contact Your Soul's Greatest Teachers.* Carlsbad, CA: Hay House, Inc., 2017.

White, Ruth. *Working with Spirit Guides.* London: Piatkus, 2004.

White, Ruth. *Working with Guides and Angels.* London: Piatkus, 1996.

About the Author

Born in Indiana and raised in Florida, Carol first earned a degree in voice and then went on to complete a Masters' of Divinity Degree with specialties in Pastoral Counseling and Spiritual Formation and a Masters' Degree in Religion. She then pursued graduate studies in New York City in the fields of Ethics and Women in American Church History.

From the late 1980's through 2006, Carol found fulfillment in employment in the areas of child welfare, domestic violence and staff development while continuing to have various part-time ministry positions. She was also a training consultant throughout New York State for the Department of Children and Families. Additionally, she wrote and delivered training curricula for SAGE, and the Brookdale Center on Aging.

After returning to Florida, she was engaged in full-time ministerial work in the Universal Fellowship of Metropolitan Community Churches. She has since retired and while she retains her ordination status as retired clergy, she is no longer active in professional work in churches except as an officiant at ceremonies and celebrations. Her first ordination was by the Southern Baptist Convention in the late 1970's. Her spiritual journey has led her far from her early training, vocation, and commitment, but she values those experiences as they gave her invaluable insight and skills. Her journey has been a protracted one weaving from conservative evangelical Christianity through years of various pathways of exploration to several Energy Healing modalities, all things Celtic, and various forms of Shamanism.

She is a Level Three Reiki practitioner, a certified Animal Reiki practitioner, and a Shamanic Practitioner. She is an artist, poet, writer, public speaker, musician, and an active blogger at www.thetenderjourney.

com. She lives in The Villages, Florida, with little Finian, her constant companion dog. She is a proud mother of one son and daughter-in-law, and a happy grandmother of two delightful grandchildren.

She is also a survivor of a life-time of mental illness and has explored the relationship between mental illness and spirituality for decades. She has been in recovery from prescription drug abuse and alcoholism for over 30 years.

She invites you to visit her webpage at www.thetenderjourney.com to leave comments regarding this book and subscribe to her mailing list so that you will get updates on her projects and events and receive her blog postings.

Thank you for sharing the experience of this journey with me.

May we all journey on in wisdom, beauty, truth, and peace. Namaste, Carol

Endnotes

1 https://www.psychiatry.org/patients-families/what-is-mental-illness.

2 Gerry C. Stearns, *Power Animals: The Role of Spirit Guides in Shamanic Journey*. (Austin, TX, SkyDance Ventures), Kindle, Loc. 115.

3 Maxwell Maltz. *Psycho-cybernetics*, (New York, Penguin, various publication dates).

4 Parker J. Palmer, *Let Your Life Speak*, (San Francisco, John Wiley & Sons, 2000), 55

5 Carrie Fisher. *Wishful Drinking* (Simon & Schuster Paperbacks, 2009)

6 Elisabeth Kubler-Ross, quoted in *Desmond Tutu, The Book of Forgiving: The Fourfold Path for Healing Ourselves and Our World*, (New York, Harper One, 2015).

7 Rachael Naomi Remen, *Kitchen Table Wisdom: Stories that Heal*, (Riverhead Books, 10th Anniversary edition, 2006).

8 Kay Redfield Jamison, *An Unquiet Mind: A Memoir of Moods and Madness*, (Vintage, 2009), Kindle.

9 Joseph Campbell with Bill Moyers, *The Power of Myth*, (New York: Anchor Books, 1991), 1.

10 Gerald G. May, *The Dark Night of the Soul: A Psychiatrist Explores the Connection Between Darkness and Spiritual Growth*, (San Francisco: Harper, 2005) 8-9.

11 Parker Palmer, *A Hidden Wholeness: The Journey Toward an Undivided Life*, (San Francisco: Josey-Bass, 2004), 5.

12 Ruth White, *Energy Healing for Beginners*, 15-16.

13 Dale, Cyndi. *Subtle Energy Techniques*. Woodbury, MN: Llewellyn Publications, 201729

14 Adapted from Ruth White, *Working with Your Chakras*, 22-24.

15 Ruth White, *Working with Your Chakras: A Physical, Emotional & Spiritual Approach*, (York Beach, ME: Samuel Weiser Inc, 1993), 106-107.

16 Ruth White, *Working with Your Chakras*, 117-118.

17 Ruth White, *Working with Your Chakras*, 87-88.

18 Ambika Wauters, *Chakras and Their Archetypes: Uniting Energy Awareness and Spiritual Growth*, (Freedom, CA: The Crossing Press, 1997), 16.

19 Ambika Wauters, *Chakras and Their Archetypes*, 27.

20 Samson, Anne. 'Reiki Leads Us on Our True Life Path', *Reiki*. Winter 2017, volume 16, Issue Four, p. 18

21 William Lee Rand, *Reiki for a New Millennium*. Rand, (Smithfield, MI: Vision Publications, 1998), 5.

22 https://www.reiki.org/FAQ/WhatIsReiki.html

23 Lisa Powers, *Reiki: Level I, II and Master Manual*, (No publisher. 2016) 9.

24 Tanmaya Honervogt, *The Power of Reiki: An Ancient Hands-On Healing Technique*, (New York, NY: St. Martin's Griffin, 1998), 38.

25 Samson, Anne. 'Reiki Leads Us on Our True Life Path', *Reiki*. Winter 2017, volume 16, Issue Four, p. 18

26 Van Der Hoeven, Joanna, *The Awen Alone: Walking the Path of the Solitary Druid*, (Alresford, Hants, UK: Moon Books, 2014, 14, Kindle.

27 Van Der Hoeven, Joanna, *The Awen Alone: Walking the Path of the Solitary Druid*, 15.

28 Frank MacEöwen, *The Mist-Filled Path*, xxiv.

29 Frank MacFöwen, *The Celtic Way of Seeing: Meditations on the Irish Spirit Wheel.* (Novato, CA: New World Library, 2007), 99.

30 Mara Freeman, *Kindling the Celtic Spirit,* (San Francisco, CA: Harper, 2001), 132.

31 Frank MacEowen, *The Mist-Filled Path: Celtic Wisdom for Exiles, Wanderers, and Seekers,* (Novato, CA: New World Library, 2002), 11.

32 Ted Andrews, *The Intercession of Spirits: Working with Animals, Angels & Ancestors,* (Jackson, TN., Dragonhawk Publishing, 2008), 29.

33 Mara Freeman, *Kindling the Celtic Spirit,* (San Francisco, CA: Harper, 2001), 191-192.

34 Sentier, Elen. *The Celtic Chakras.* Winchester, UK: Moon Books, 2013.

35 http://www.dailyom.com/cgi-bin/display/librarydisplay.cgi?lid=3079

36 Mara Freeman, *Kindling the Celtic Spirit,* (San Francisco, CA: Harper, 2001), 5.

37 Frank MacEowen, *The Mist-Filled Path: Celtic Wisdom for Exiles, Wanderers, and Seekers,* (Novato, CA: New World Library, 2002), 12-14.

38 Ted Andrews, *The Intercession of Spirits: Working with Animals, Angels & Ancestors,* (Jackson, TN., Dragonhawk Publishing, 2008), 225.

39 Ted Andrews, *The Intercession of Spirits: Working with Animals, Angels & Ancestors,* (Jackson, TN. Dragonhawk Publishing, 2008), 29.

40 Garrett, Michael T., *Walking on the Wind: Cherokee Teaching for Harmony and Balance,* (Sante Fe, NM: Bear & Company, 1998), 16.

41 Garrett, Michael T., *Walking on the Wind,* 18.

42 Michael T. Garrett, *Walking on the Wind,* 18.

43 Michael T. Garrett, *Walking on the Wind,* 23, 26

44 Jim Pathfinder Ewing, https://www.manataka.org/page694.html.

45 Black Elk Quoted in Michael T. Garrett, *Walking on the Wind,* 75.

46 Jim Pathfinder Ewing, https://www.manataka.org/page694.html.

47 Michael T. Garrett, *Walking on the Wind,* 100.

48 Jamie Sams, *Dancing the Dream: The Seven Sacred Paths of Human Transformation,* (New York, NY: Harper Collins, 1998), 18.

49 J.T. Garrett and Michael Garrett. *Medicine of the Cherokee: The Way of Right Relationship.* (Rochester, VT: Bear & Company, 1996), 99.

50 J.T. Garrett and Michael Garrett. *Medicine of the Cherokee,* 110.

51 J.T. Garrett and Michael Garrett. *Medicine of the Cherokee,* 131.

52 J.T. Garrett and Michael Garrett. *Medicine of the Cherokee,* 132.

53 Anna Dorian. https://vibrantreiki.com/Shamanism/

54 Meaning I have not apprenticed myself to any indigenous Shamanism for intense study

55 D. J. Conway, *By Oak, Ash, & Thorn: Modern Celtic Shamanism,* (Woodbury, MN: Llewellyn Worldwide, 2017), 3-4.

56 D. J. Conway, *By Oak, Ash, & Thorn: Modern Celtic Shamanism,* (Woodbury, MN: Llewellyn Worldwide, 2017), 15

57 John Matthews, *The Shamanism Bible,* (Buffalo, N.Y.: Firefly Books, 2014, 213.

58 Sandra Ingerman, and Hank Wesselman, *Awakening to the Spirit World: The Shamanic Path of Direct Revelation* (Boulder, CO: Sounds True, 2010), 9-10.

59 Alberto Villoldo, *Mending the Past and Healing the Future with Soul Retrieval,* (Carlsbad, CO: Hay House, 2005), xii.

60 Sandra Ingerman, and Hank Wesselman, xvii, xviii, xix.

61 Sandra Ingerman, and Hank Wesselman, *Awakening to the Spirit World*, 13,14.

62 Sandra Ingerman, *Soul Retrieval: Mending the Fragmented Self*, (New York: Harper One, 1991), 202.

63 Colleen Deatsman, *The Hollow Bone: A Field Guide to Shamanism*, (San Francisco, CA, Weiser Books, 2011) 62.

64 J.A. Kent, *The Goddess and The Shamanism: The Art and Science of Magical Healing*, (Woodbury, MN: Llewellyn Publications, 2016), xxi.

65 Malidoma Patrice Somé, *Ritual: Power, Healing, and Community*, (New York, NY: Penguin, 1993), 67.

66 Sandra Ingerman, and Hank Wesselman, *Awakening to the Spirit World: The Shamanic Path of Direct Revelation* (Boulder, CO: Sounds True, 2010), 7.

67 Sandra Ingerman, *Soul Retrieval: Mending the Fragmented Self*, (New York: Harper One, 1991), 34-36.

68 Sandra Ingerman, and Hank Wesselman, *Awakening to the Spirit World: The Shamanic Path of Direct Revelation* (Boulder, CO: Sounds True, 2010), 32-34.

69 R.J. Stewart, R.J., ed. *Psychology & the Spiritual Traditions*. (Longmead, Shaftesbury, Dorset, UK: Element Books, 1999), 63.

70 Mike Williams, *Follow the Shamanism's Call: An Ancient Path for Modern Lives*, (Woodbury, MN, Llewellyn Publishers, 2010), 203,

71 D. J. Conway, *By Oak, Ash, & Thorn: Modern Celtic Shamanism*, (Woodbury, MN: Llewellyn Worldwide, 2017), 53.

72 Stephen V. Beyer, Foreword in Howard G. Charing, *The Accidental Shamanism: Journeys with Plant Teachers and Other Spirit Allies*, (Rochester, VT: Destiny Books, 2017), ix.

73 Sandra Ingerman, *Soul Retrieval: Mending the Fragmented Self*, (New York: Harper One, 1991), 11,14.

74 Caitlín Matthews, *Singing the Soul Back Home: Shamanic Wisdom for Every Day*, (U.S.A., Connections Book Publishing, 2002), 226,227.

75 Kathryn Skaggs, Presentation at The Villages, FL, 2/14/18.

76 Interview with Christina Pratt with "Why Shamanism Now", http://whyshamanismnow.com/2018/10/teens-shamanism-and-hidden-worlds-with-sandra-ingerman/, October 30, 2018.

77 Howard G. Charing, *The Accidental Shamanism: Journeys with Plant Teachers and Other Spirit Allies*, (Rochester, VT: Destiny Books, 2017), 45,46.

78 Alberto Villoldo, *Mending the Past and Healing the Future with Soul Retrieval*, (Carlsbad, CO: Hay House, 2005), 30.

79 Osho, *Beloved of my Heart* in Honervogt

80 Sentier, Elen, *The Celtic Chakras*, (Winchester, UK: Moon Books, 2013), 61-62.

81 Dianne M. Connelly, *All Sickness is Home Sickness: An Inspiring Book about Illness, Healing, and Living*. (Unknown Publisher, 1993), 114.

82 https://www.thetenderjourney.com/single-post/2018/11/12/Hope

83 Deena Metzger. This quote appears in many blogs and websites on the internet. However, I was unable to find the original source.

84 Dianne M. Connelly, *All Sickness is Home Sickness: An Inspiring Book about Illness, Healing, and Living*. (Unknown Publisher, 1993), 172.

85 Sandra Ingerman, *Walking in the Light: the Everyday Empowerment of a Shamanic Life*, 4, Kindle.

86 Deena Metzger, *Illness Heals the World*, http://deenametzger.net/illness-heals-the-world/.